EASY
Japanese
QUILT STYLE

EASY
Japanese
QUILT STYLE

Julia Davis & Anne Muxworthy

D&C
David and Charles

www.mycraftivity.com

A DAVID & CHARLES BOOK
Copyright © David & Charles Limited 2009

David & Charles is an F+W Media Inc. company
4700 East Galbraith Road
Cincinnati, OH 45236

First published in the UK and USA in 2009
Reprinted in 2009, 2010 (twice)

Text and illustrations copyright © Julia Davis and
Anne Muxworthy 2009

Photographs copyright © David & Charles Limited 2009

A catalogue record for this book is available from the British Library.

ISBN-13: 978-0-7153-2862-0 paperback
ISBN-10: 0-7153-2862-X paperback

Printed in China by RR Donnelley
for David & Charles
Brunel House   Newton Abbot   Devon

Commissioning Editor: Jane Trollope
Desk Editor: Emily Rae
Art Editor: Sarah Clark
Designer: Sabine Eulau
Production Controller: Kelly Smith
Photographers: Kim Sayer and Karl Adamson

David & Charles publish high quality books on a wide range
of subjects.
For more great book ideas visit: www.rucraft.co.uk

Contents

Introduction

When we were first shown these beautiful fabrics some six or seven years ago, we both fell in love with the amazing colours and designs. It was difficult to know what not to buy; they were all so sumptuous with the gold outlining and stunning flower designs, ribbons and fans. The blender fabrics are essential additions to the main fabrics and are beautiful in their own right. The limited collections are also wonderful with their large and bold prints. Even today, the fabrics are still amazing us and are becoming more gorgeous with every collection.

Despite being bright and bold, Oriental style fabrics can be mixed together for a very pleasing effect, whether you are making a bag, wallhanging or a bed quilt. Just bear in mind that, at some juncture, it is nice to define your work with a simpler border or binding. This can be achieved either with a blender fabric that has a tone of the colours you have used or else a complete contrast.

The quality of the fabrics is a key factor and we have found that they cut well, press easily and are a joy to sew. We love thinking up new ideas for using these fabrics to their best effect, which can be a challenge, particularly with the larger prints. The six inch (15.2cm) squares illustrated and used on projects in this book are from the Oriental Charm Pack that we produce and is available from Step By Step Patchwork Centre (see Suppliers, page 126).

We hope that this book will inspire you, as the fabrics we use have inspired us. Enjoy.

Yonjuu Sankaku Bag

This cunningly constructed bag is a great way
to use up charm squares or leftover fabrics.
The name literally translates to '40 triangles'.
The tried and tested 'windmill' construction
means that you don't have to insert the base of
this surprisingly capacious bag. Ties with fabric
beads give the bag a different decorative finish.

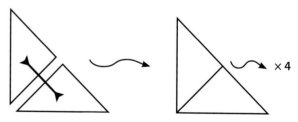

WHAT YOU NEED

- Twenty 6in (15.2cm) squares of various prints and tonal fabrics
- 20in x 44in (50cm x 112cm) lining fabric
- One 2½in x 44in (6.3cm x 112cm) strip for binding
- Two 4in x 20in (10cm x 50cm) strips for handles
- Four 2in x 12in (5cm x 30.4cm) strips for ties
- Four 3in x 2in (7.5cm x 5cm) rectangles for fabric beads
- 20in x 44in (50cm x 112cm) wadding

Finished size: 10in x 10in x 10in (25cm x 25cm x 25cm)

Construction

1 Cut each of the 20 squares in half diagonally to produce 40 triangles (diagram **a**).

2 Arrange in groups of four (diagram **b**) and sew together using a ¼in (6mm) seam. Line up your centre seams as best as possible.

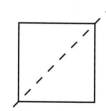

3 Sew the remaining eight triangles together to produce four larger half square triangles (diagram **c**).

4 Using two full squares and one half square triangle, make up four identical sections (diagram **d**). Layer each section with a piece of wadding and machine quilt together.

5 At this stage, using your patchwork sections as a template, cut out four lining pieces by placing the sections right sides together with the lining fabric.

TIP

To save yourself from marking the patchwork when machine quilting the four identical sections, follow the seam lines with a straight stitch either side of the seam to produce 'tram lines'. Or, if you want an opportunity to play with your machine, use a fancy machine stitch.

6 Now join the patchwork sections together at the centre, using the windmill configuration shown in diagram **d**.

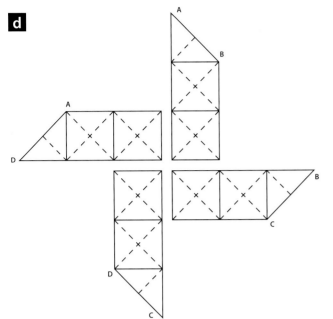

7 Using a good ¼in (6mm) seam, join A to A, B to B, C to C and D to D as indicated in diagram **d**.

8 Repeat this joining sequence for the lining.

9 Place the lining inside the bag with wrong sides facing and tack the top edges of the patchwork and lining fabrics together. The binding strip should be ironed in half along its length (wrong sides together). Fold in one end by ¼in (6mm) to neaten. Place the raw edges of the binding against the outside raw edge of the bag and sew in place. Turn the folded edge to the inside of the bag and hand sew in place.

Making the handles

Fold each of the 4in x 20in (10cm x 50cm) strips in half along their length. Seam together down one long edge, turn inside out and iron so that the seam lies through the centre. Reinforce by feeding a 1¼in (3.2cm) strip of wadding through the handle and sewing with multiple rows of top stitching (see detail, right). Fold under the handle ends to neaten and top stitch securely in place (diagram **e**).

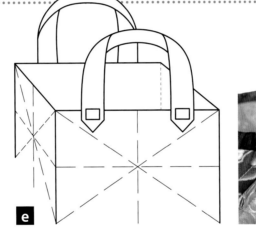

Making the ties

Fold the 2in x 12in (5cm x 30.4cm) strips in half along their length, right sides together, and stitch a ¼in (6mm) seam. Turn right sides out and press. Top stitch. Fold one end on each tie back by ½in (1.3cm) and sew in place as shown in diagram **f**.

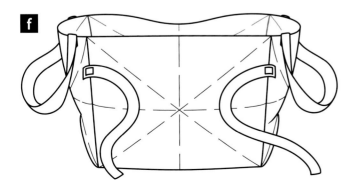

Making the fabric beads

1 Fold each 2in x 3in (5cm x 7.5cm) rectangle in half, right sides together, down their length to produce a 2in x 1½in (5cm x 3.8cm) rectangle.

2 Sew a ¼in (6mm) seam securing both ends. Sew a gathering stitch around one end of this tube leaving the thread attached (diagram **g**).

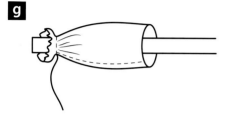

g

3 Now feed the tie end through the tube so that the raw edge comes out just beyond the gathered end. Pull the thread up so that it gathers up tightly around the tie end. Fasten very securely. Now bring back the open end of the tube over the tie end to reveal the right side of the fabric (diagram **h**).

h

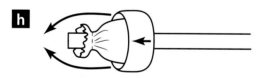

4 Turn in ½in (1.3cm) of fabric to neaten the end, stuff with wadding and secure the end as in diagram **i**. Repeat for the other three ties. Knot the ties together to draw in the bag ends.

i

Stuff

Gather tightly

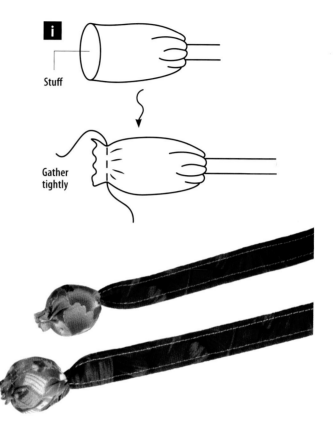

FABRIC CHOICE

This bag looks appealing in many colour ways. Try picking fabrics with a colour theme to suit the season it will be used in – warm reds and golds for autumn, light florals for spring and summer or more practical blues and purples for winter.

Think how lovely it would be to make one from Christmas fabrics as a gift to a dear friend.

The Hoko Bag

The patchwork Yonjuu Sankaku Bag (pages 8–12) is great fun to make using lots of different fabrics, but this alternative or hoko (meaning 'other') version is made with just two main fabrics and is much quicker to construct. The addition of fabric flowers gives it a lovely summer appeal.

WHAT YOU NEED

- Two thin quarters (25cm) of coordinating fabric (fabric A and B)
- 20in x 44in (50cm x 112cm) lining fabric
- 20in x 44in (50cm x 112cm) wadding
- One 2½in x 44in (6.3cm x 112cm) strip for binding
- Two 4in x 20in (10cm x 50cm) strips for handles
- Four 2in x 12in (5cm x 30.4cm) strips for ties
- Four 3in x 2in (7.5cm x 5cm) rectangles for fabric beads
- Six 5½in (14cm) circles of varying colours for flowers
- Six ¾in (2cm) buttons
- Eight 3in (7.5cm) squares green fabric for leaves

Finished size: 10in x 10in x 10in (25cm x 25cm x 25cm)

Construction

1 Make a template for the bag panels from thin card, using the dimensions given in diagram **a**.

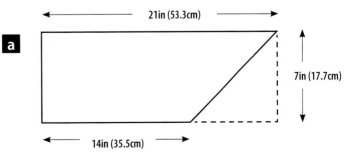

a

21in (53.3cm)

7in (17.7cm)

14in (35.5cm)

2 From this template cut two panels from fabric A and two panels from fabric B (diagram **b**).

Fabric A

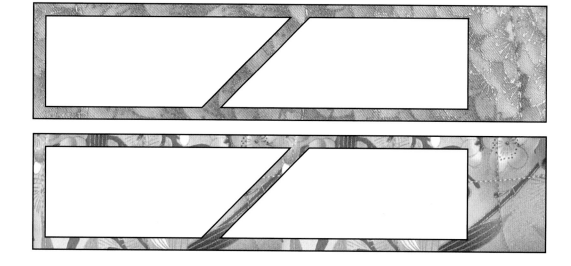

Fabric B

3 From the lining fabric cut four panels using the same template but in reverse.

4 Layer each of the outer fabric panels with wadding and tack together, or use temporary spray adhesive.

5 Quilt the panels either by hand or machine. We have cross-hatch quilted the panels in lines 2in (5cm) apart (see diagram **c**).

6 Trim excess wadding.

7 Now carry on constructing your bag as from step 6 of the Yonjuu Sankaku Bag on page 11.

c

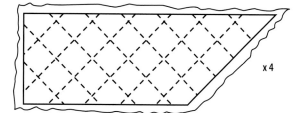

x 4

Making the flowers

1 Turn the edge of a 5½in (14cm) circle by ⅛in (4mm). Sew a line of small running stitches around this neatened edge – pull up the thread to gather the edges together as close as possible. Securely fasten off. You now have a Suffolk puff or yo-yo.

2 To create the petals, run another line of small running stitches from the centre to the edge of your yo-yo. Pull up and fasten. Repeat until you have created five petals (see diagram **d**). Repeat steps 1 and 2 until you have six flowers.

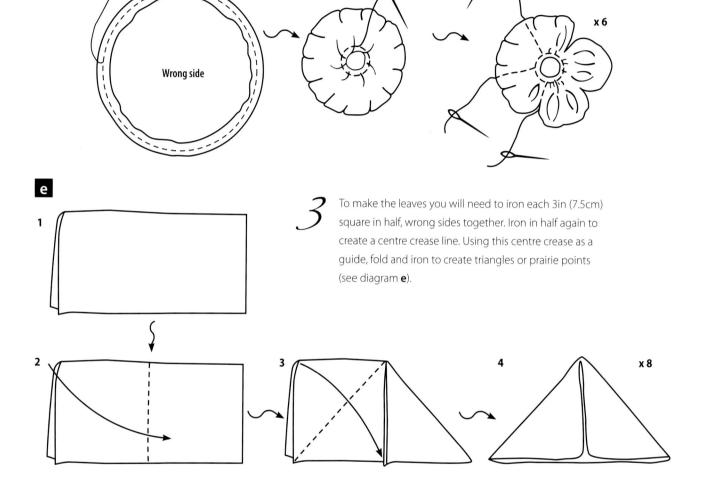

3 To make the leaves you will need to iron each 3in (7.5cm) square in half, wrong sides together. Iron in half again to create a centre crease line. Using this centre crease as a guide, fold and iron to create triangles or prairie points (see diagram **e**).

4 fold the two corners towards the middle, gather the edge, and fasten off securely. Repeat for all eight leaves (diagram **f**).

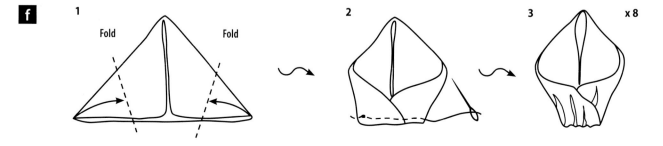

5 Sew the flowers and leaves to the bag along the diagonal seam on the sides where the handles are attached (diagram **g**). Sew a button to each flower centre.

g

TIP

Yo-yos are quite simple to make in the way we have described in step 1, but you can speed up the process even further by using a yo-yo maker. Just follow the manufacturer's instructions on how to use.

It is so easy to change the look of the bag just by using different fabrics for the flowers. Choose buttons that pick out colours in the bag fabrics.

Karesansui Table Mats and Runner

These very simple, yet stylish, table mats and matching runner will look good on your table whatever the occasion, whether it be a formal dinner party or a casual Sunday breakfast.

'Karesansui' translates as waterless rock and sand and the colours chosen depict exactly that – the dark lines form the rocks and the cream, with its delicate quilting, the sand, in a Zen garden.

WHAT YOU NEED

- 50in (127cm) main fabric
- 34in (86.5cm) accent fabric
- 30in (76cm) Insul Bright wadding or similar
- Mettler waxed hand quilting thread

Cutting instructions

Main fabric:

- six 9½in x 9¾in (24cm x 24.7cm)
- twelve 2in x 9¾in (5cm x 24.7cm)
- six 2in x 14in (5cm x 35.5cm)
- eight 2½in x 44in (6.3cm x 112cm)
- two 1¼in x 2in (3.2cm x 5cm)

Accent fabric:

- twelve 1¼in x 9¾in (3.2cm x 24.7cm)
- six 1¼in x 14in (3.2cm x 35.5cm)
- one 1¼in x 9in (3.2cm x 23cm)

Finished size: mats 14in x 11½in (35.5cm x 29cm); runner 28in x 11½in (71cm x 29cm)

Construction

1 With each of your six 9½in x 9¾in (24cm x 24.7cm) main fabric pieces, join a 1¼in x 9¾in (3.2cm x 24.7cm) accent fabric to the right side. Then join a 2in x 9¾in (5cm x 24.7cm) main fabric piece to the right side of this. Repeat this once more. Press all seams and square up (see diagram **a**).

TIP
Insul Bright wadding is not the easiest to hand quilt but it does make for bigger stitches.

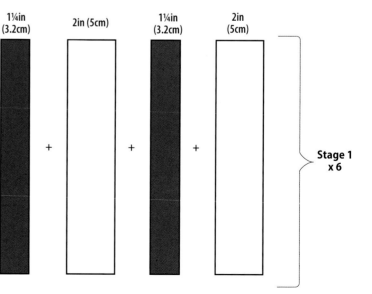

a

9½in (24cm)

1¼in (3.2cm) 2in (5cm) 1¼in (3.2cm) 2in (5cm)

9¾in (24.7cm)

\+ \+ \+

Stage 1 x 6

2 Take the six 1¼in x 14in (3.2cm x 35.5cm) accent fabric
strips and sew to the top edge of each piece, then add the
final 2in x 14in (5cm x 35.5cm) main fabric strips. Trim and
press (see diagram **b**).

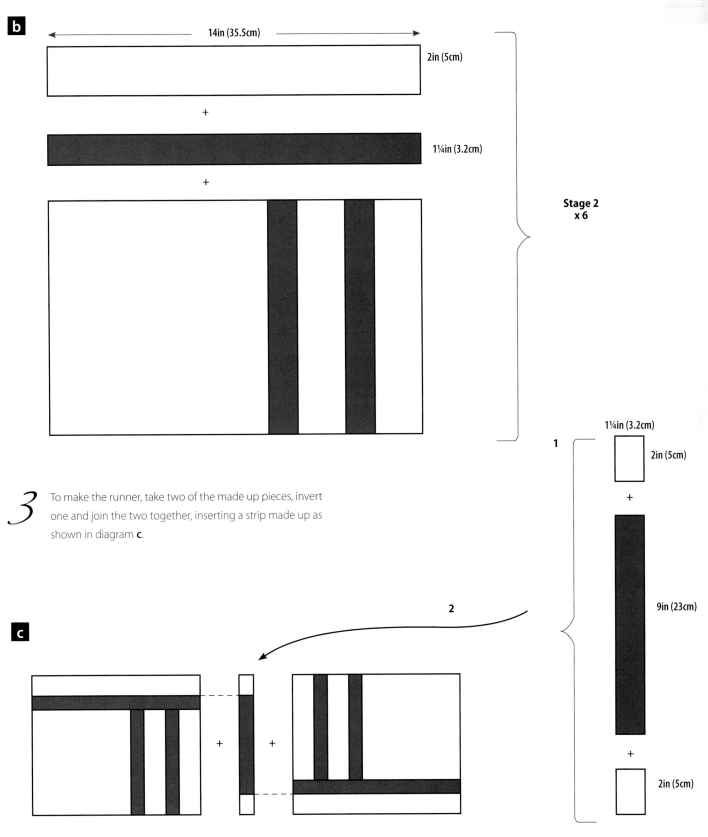

b

14in (35.5cm)

2in (5cm)

+

1¼in (3.2cm)

+

**Stage 2
x 6**

3 To make the runner, take two of the made up pieces, invert
one and join the two together, inserting a strip made up as
shown in diagram **c**.

1

1¼in (3.2cm)

2in (5cm)

+

9in (23cm)

+

2in (5cm)

2

c

+   +

4 Now with the four mats and runner tops completed, layer with wadding and backing. Quilt as shown in diagram **d**.

d

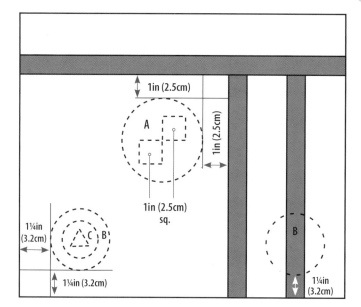

1in (2.5cm)

1in (2.5cm)

A

1in (2.5cm)
sq.

1¼in
(3.2cm)

C B

1¼in (3.2cm)

B

1¼in
(3.2cm)

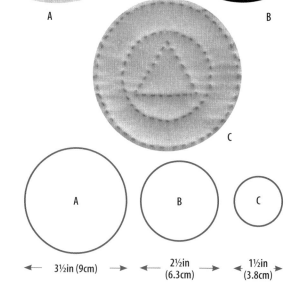

A

B

C

A   B   C

← 3½in (9cm) → ← 2½in (6.3cm) → ← 1½in (3.8cm) →

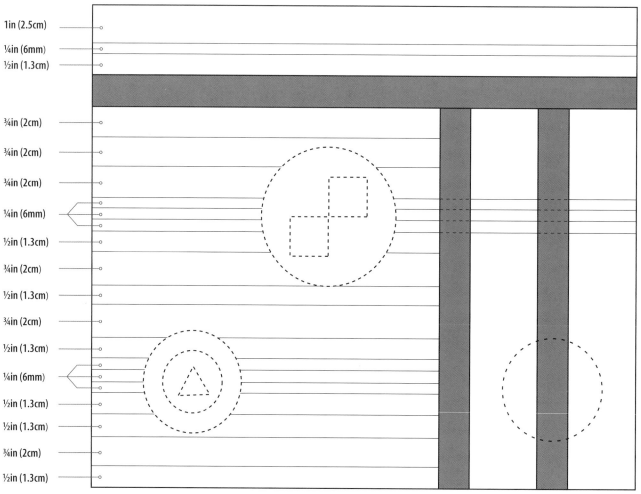

1in (2.5cm)
¼in (6mm)
½in (1.3cm)

¾in (2cm)

¾in (2cm)

¾in (2cm)

¼in (6mm)

½in (1.3cm)

¾in (2cm)

½in (1.3cm)

¾in (2cm)

½in (1.3cm)

¼in (6mm)

½in (1.3cm)

½in (1.3cm)

¾in (2cm)

½in (1.3cm)

5 Trim all the edges and bind according to the instructions on pages 114–115.

instructions on pages 114–115.

TIP

We marked the quilting lines with a blue washaway pen. If you make a drafting mistake it is easily removed with water. Always rinse in clear water when quilting is complete.

FABRIC CHOICE

This is a simple project and so you should keep your fabrics simple as well. Use only two colours, keeping your main fabric lighter and the contrast of a dark value. It is not necessary to use a taupe, although this does have a very pleasing effect. If your dining room is decorated in different colours, match the mats with the nearest light and dark in that room.

As a colour alternative, you could use traditional sashiko fabric, which is a dark or navy blue and the quilting can then be either cream or white, using sashiko thread, which can look very striking. You will achieve a thicker quilting stitch.

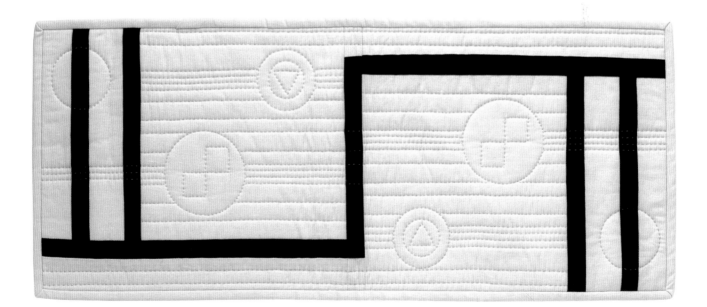

The table runner is an understated but striking design with its geometric shapes. Varying the depth of the quilted lines and including the circles adds to the interest.

Sakura Sewing Set

Sakura, or cherry blossom, features heavily in many Oriental designs so it seemed an obvious choice to use a stylized version of this lovely flower as the theme for this sewing set. With matching pincushion, needle case and scissor holder, it would make a beautiful and practical gift for a friend who loves sewing – or an attractive addition to your own sewing kit.

Sakura Pincushion

This pretty yet extremely useful pincushion could be made
as a gift for a sewing friend in their favourite colours.
All the pieces of fabric could easily be found in your 'bits' box.

WHAT YOU NEED

- Fat quarter for petals and base
- 6in (15.2cm) square for centre
- Two 6in (15.2cm) squares for leaves
  (can be two different greens)
- Small quantity of wadding for petals and leaves
- Toy stuffing
- 15 small pearl beads
- 2in (5cm) circle of card
- 2½in (6.3cm) circle of wadding

Finished size: 6½in x 4in x 2in (16.5cm x 10cm x 5cm)

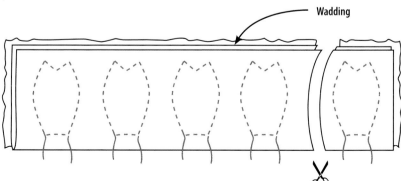

Construction

1 To make the petals, fold the fat quarter in half, right sides
together, and draw five times around the petal template
on page 120 , leaving a seam allowance around each one.
Lay the folded fat quarter on to the wadding and sew
around each petal on your drawn line through all the
layers, as shown in diagram **a**. Cut out each petal ¼in
(6mm) from the sewing line.

a Wadding

b

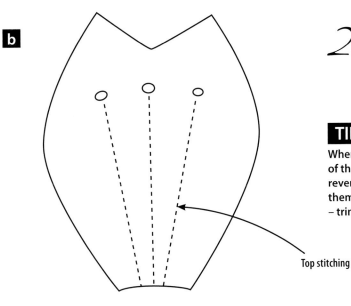

2 Clip the corners, trim the wadding back to your seam line and turn inside out. Press. Top stitch as shown in diagram **b** and sew a pearl bead at the top of each line.

Top stitching

3 Now take the 6in (15.2cm) centre square fabric and cut a 5½in (14cm) circle. Starting with a substantial knot and a back stitch, run a line of gathering stitches ¼in (6mm) in from the edge. Pull up the thread and pack firmly with toy stuffing. Anchor the end well.

4 Position and pin the petals around the edge of the stuffed circle (bead side facing inwards) as in diagram **c**. There should be a 2in (5cm) gap on the base between the petals. Slip stitch the base of the petals in place. Draw the petals up so that they slightly overlap each other and place a securing stitch ¾in (2cm) up from the base so that they remain upright around the stuffed centre.

c

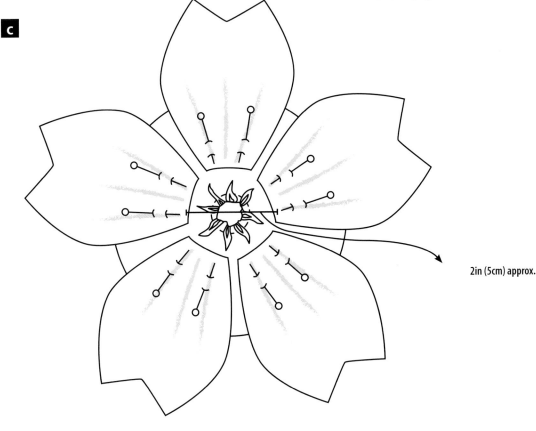

2in (5cm) approx.

5 Using the leaf template on page 120, make three leaves, using the same method as for the petals. We have used two different greens for these, a lighter tone for the underside of the leaves, darker for the fronts. Top stitch through all layers to give the impression of a central vein. Position these as in diagram **d**. Slip stitch in place and put a securing stitch at each side of a leaf, ¾in (2cm) up from the base.

d

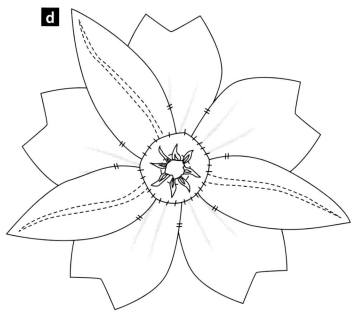

6 To cover the base, cut a 3in (7.5cm) circle of the petal fabric and run a line of gathering stitches around the edge. Place wrong side up. Put a 2½in (6.3cm) circle of wadding and a 2in (5cm) circle of card on to the base circle and draw up the gathering thread around the wadding and card. With the card side facing the base, position over all the raw edges of the petals and leaves and slip stitch in place.

Sakura Needle Case

This needle case has enough felt pages to house a good selection of needle sizes and the side pockets are the right size to keep new packs of needles.

WHAT YOU NEED

- Two 5in x 11in (12.5cm x 28cm) rectangles for outer and lining
- One 5in x 11in (12.5cm x 28cm) rectangle of wadding
- 34in (86.5cm) of 1½in (3.8cm) binding
- Two 6in (15.2cm) squares for sakura flower
- One 6in (15.2cm) square of wadding for flower
- One 3in x 6½in (7.5cm x 16.5cm) rectangle for pocket A
- One 3in x 5½in (7.5cm x 14cm) rectangle for pocket B
- Four 4½in x 4in (11.5cm x 10cm) rectangles of felt
- 15 small pearl beads
- One 1in (2.5cm) button

Finished size: 5in x 5in (12.5cm x 12.5cm)

Construction

1 Layer a 5in x 11in (12.5cm x 28cm) rectangle of outer fabric with the same size piece of wadding. Machine quilt by cross-hatching at 1½in (3.8cm) intervals.

2 To make the needle packet pockets, fold in half with right sides together, as shown in diagram **a**, and sew a ¼in (6mm) seam. Clip corners and turn inside out. Press and top stitch the seamed edge. Place on to the 5in x 11in (12.5cm x 28cm) lining rectangle as shown in diagram **b** (page 30) and tack the raw edges in place.

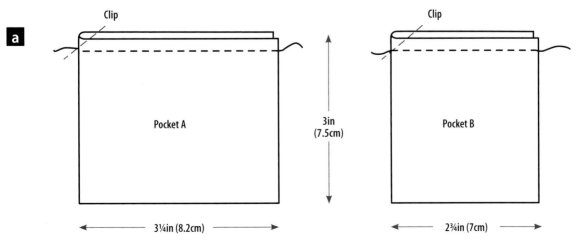

a

Clip

Pocket A

Clip

Pocket B

3in (7.5cm)

3¼in (8.2cm)

2¾in (7cm)

b

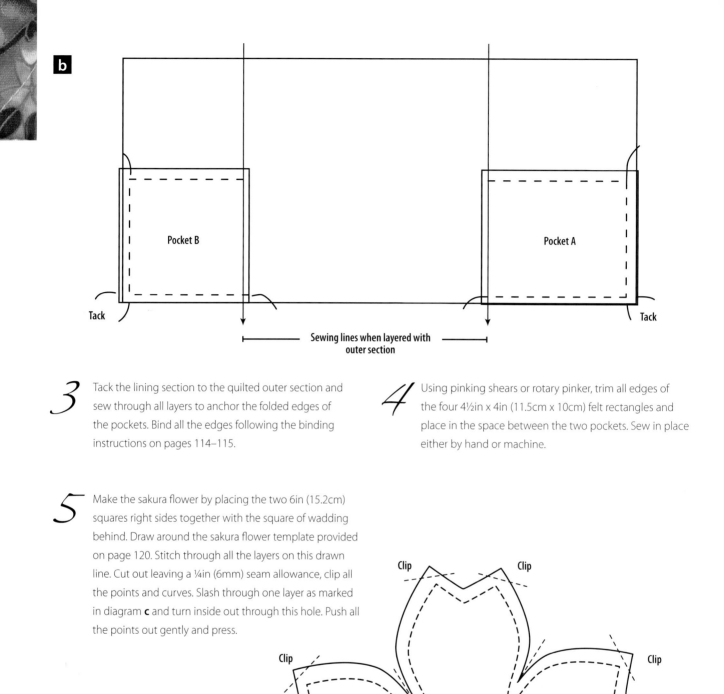

Pocket B

Pocket A

Tack

Tack

Sewing lines when layered with
outer section

3 Tack the lining section to the quilted outer section and sew through all layers to anchor the folded edges of the pockets. Bind all the edges following the binding instructions on pages 114–115.

4 Using pinking shears or rotary pinker, trim all edges of the four 4½in x 4in (11.5cm x 10cm) felt rectangles and place in the space between the two pockets. Sew in place either by hand or machine.

5 Make the sakura flower by placing the two 6in (15.2cm) squares right sides together with the square of wadding behind. Draw around the sakura flower template provided on page 120. Stitch through all the layers on this drawn line. Cut out leaving a ¼in (6mm) seam allowance, clip all the points and curves. Slash through one layer as marked in diagram **c** and turn inside out through this hole. Push all the points out gently and press.

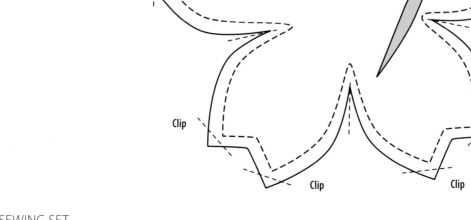

Clip

Clip

Clip

Clip

Clip

Clip

c

Slash

Clip

Clip

Clip

Clip

Clip

Clip

6 Top stitch as shown in diagram **d**. Work a buttonhole at this point, through the centre of the flower and sew a small pearl bead at the top of each sewn line, taking care with all the knots as for the pincushion. Make two leaves, using the template on page 120 and following the pincushion instructions on page 28.

d

TIP

If you don't feel confident enough to work a buttonhole, make a closure with a popper (press stud) or Velcro and sew the button to the centre of the flower.

FABRIC CHOICE

We have deliberately chosen a tone on tone fabric for the flower/petal motifs to emphasize the shapes. The main fabric for the needle case has sakura in the design for obvious effect. The overall colour theme gives the set a very feminine feel. We have just given fabric cutting requirements for each individual item of the sewing set as all the pieces are so small they should be easily found from a 'stash'.

7 With the quilted side of the needle case facing upwards, position the leaves and flower as shown in diagram **e** and slip stitch in place. Sew the button on the left hand side, approximately 1in (2.5cm) from the edge to correspond with the buttonhole.

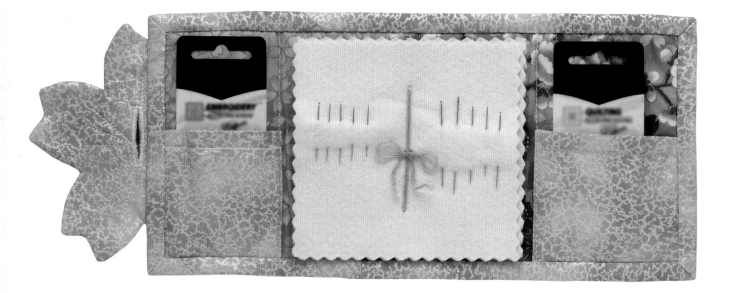

Your choice of lining material is important here – a patterned contrast to the outer fabric will make a statement every time the case is opened.

Sakura Scissors Case

Most scissors come in a plastic case when bought. This simple project not only helps to protect them but also makes a simple gift of scissors something special.

WHAT YOU NEED

- Two 4½in (11.5cm) squares feature fabric
- One 4½in (11.5cm) square wadding
- Two 3in (7.5cm) squares petal fabric
- One 3in (7.5cm) square wadding
- Two 4in x 3in (10cm x 7.5cm) rectangles for leaf
- One 4in x 3in (10cm x 7.5cm) rectangle of wadding
- One ½in (1.3cm) button
- One 2in x 1½in (5cm x 3.8cm) rectangle for bead end
- Three small pearl beads
- One large pearl bead

Finished size: 5in x 3in (12.5cm x 7.5cm)

Construction

1 Layer the two 4½in (11.5cm) feature fabric squares, right sides together and place on the 4½in (11.5cm) square of wadding. Using a ¼in (6mm) seam, sew around the edges through all layers, leaving a gap for turning. Clip the corners and turn right sides out, press and slip stitch the turning hole closed. Top stitch through all the layers around the edge.

2 Bring points D and B together, edge-to-edge and ladder stitch closed as far as point C (see diagram **a**).

a

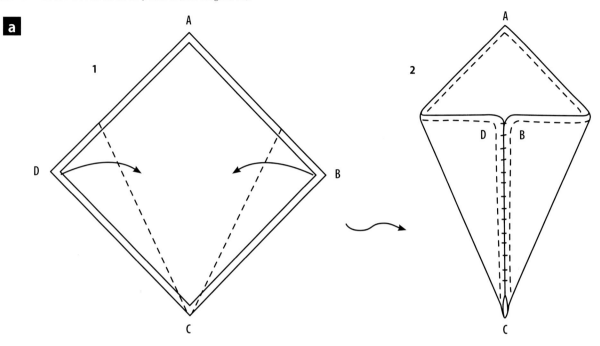

3 Make the petal flap by placing the two 3in (7.5cm) squares of petal fabric right sides together and layering with the 3in (7.5cm) square of wadding. Draw around the petal template on page 120. This drawn line is your sewing line. Cut out the petal leaving a ¼in (6mm) seam allowance. Clip all the points and curves, turn right sides out, press and top stitch as for the pincushion petals (page 27). Work a buttonhole ½in (1.3cm) in from the edge (or alternatively you can use a press stud). Add a small bead to the ends of each row of stitching.

4 To make the leaf, layer the two 4in x 3in (10cm x 7.5cm) rectangles of green fabric, right sides together, with the wadding in the middle. Draw around the leaf template on page 120 – again this drawn line is your sewing line. Cut out, clip points and curves and slash through one layer to turn right sides out. Press and run a line of gathering stitches through the centre of the leaf.

5 Now assemble as in diagram **b**, sewing the petal and leaf in place using small slip stitches.

1

1in (2.5cm)

2

6 To cover the end of the case, a fabric bead can be made using the 1½in x 2in (3.8cm x 5cm) rectangle. Fold in half and sew a scant ¼in (6mm) seam. Gather around one end and place over the point of the scissor case (diagram **c**). Pull up the gathering stitches and fasten off securely. Pull down over the point, stuff with a small amount of toy stuffing, turn up the edge by a small amount to neaten and gather together the end. Fasten off with a large pearl bead at the end.

3

4

c

1

1½in (3.8cm)

2

Stuff

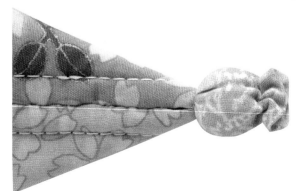

7 Lastly, sew a ½in (1.3cm) button approximately ½in (1.3cm) down from the front edge, where points D and B meet (see diagram **a**, page 35).

Sakura Pagoda Hokusai Wave Wallhanging

There are many large panels available and the dilemma usually is how to make the best use of them. Here we have taken colour elements from the panels to provide us with a palette for the patchwork borders.

WHAT YOU NEED

- One 24in (60cm) repeat panel from a large print design
- Twelve 6in (15.2cm) squares of coordinating fabric
- 39¼in (1m) of white on white/neutral fabric
- Thin quarter (25cm) for binding
- 47in (1.2m) backing fabric
- Wadding 36in x 46in (91.4cm x 117cm) e.g. Thermolam or Armofleece

Cutting instructions

White on white fabric:
- seven 1½in x 44in (3.8cm x 112cm) strips
- one 10in x 25in (25cm x 63.5cm) rectangle
- sixteen 6in (15.2cm) squares

Thin quarter:
- four 2½in x 44in (6.3cm x 112cm) strips for binding

Finished size: 44in (112cm) high x 34in (86.5cm) wide

Construction

1 From your large print panel, cut a rectangle 21½in (54.6cm) wide by 23½in (59.7cm) long.

2 Pair up each of the twelve 6in (15.2cm) patterned squares with a white 6in (15.2cm) square, right sides facing. Draw a line diagonally from corner to corner on each white square. Sew a good ¼in (6mm) seam either side of this line through both layers. Cut in half along the original centre line. Iron seams to the patterned fabric. Now cut each half square triangle diagonally in half again. See diagram **a**, where pink represents patterned fabric and plain represents white.

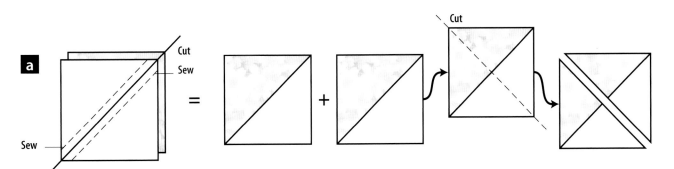

3 Using 12 of these smaller units, make up six squares as shown in diagram **b**. Join these together to make a strip.

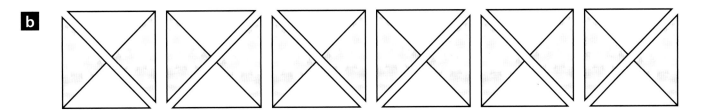

4 Trim each strip of squares as shown in diagram **c**, leaving a ¼in (6mm) seam allowance beyond the end points. Repeat this sequence to produce four pieced strips in all.

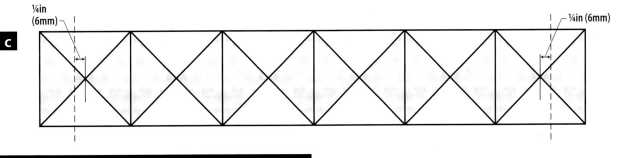

TIP

When making up the six squares in step 2, make sure to trim all of your squares so that they are all the same size.

5 Add a 1½in (3.8cm) white strip to each vertical side of the centre panel. Press seams to the white fabric. Add a pieced strip to each of these sides and continue adding strips/borders as shown in diagram **d**. Trim top corners and base segment (diagram **e**).

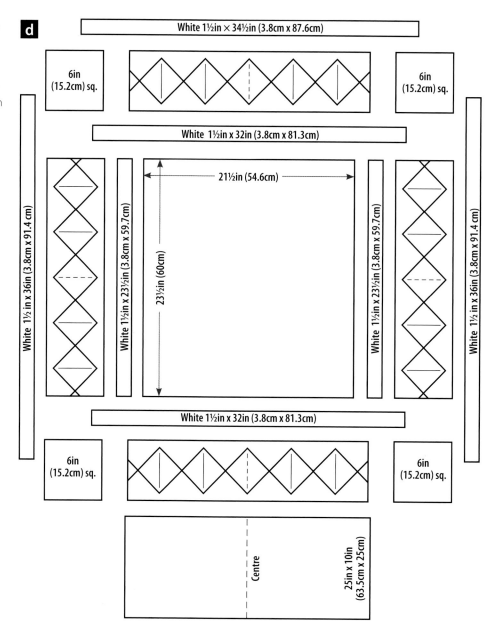

d

White 1½in × 34½in (3.8cm x 87.6cm)

6in (15.2cm) sq.

6in (15.2cm) sq.

White 1½in x 32in (3.8cm x 81.3cm)

White 1½ in x 36in (3.8cm x 91.4 cm)

White 1½in x 23½in (3.8cm x 59.7cm)

21½in (54.6cm)

23½in (60cm)

White 1½in x 23½in (3.8cm x 59.7cm)

White 1½ in x 36in (3.8cm x 91.4 cm)

White 1½in x 32in (3.8cm x 81.3cm)

6in (15.2cm) sq.

6in (15.2cm) sq.

Centre

25in x 10in (63.5cm x 25cm)

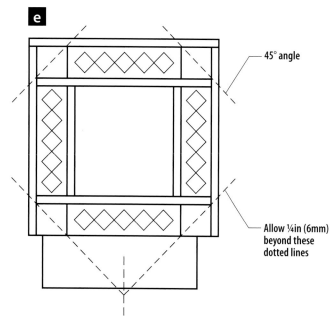

e

45° angle

Allow ¼in (6mm) beyond these dotted lines

6 Appliqué a suitable motif from another large print fabric on to the base triangle using any fusible web such as Bondaweb.

7 Now layer your pieced top with your wadding and backing fabric and tack all layers together securely. Quilt, making sure that the appliquéd motif is stitched in place.

8 Finally, bind all edges and add a hanging sleeve at the top and two further sleeves as shown in diagram **f**, to accommodate thin battons or canes to stop the edges from curling forward.

FABRIC CHOICE

Fabrics with large repeat patterns of approximately 24in (60cm) are ideal for these projects. Use white self-patterned fabrics for the background to give a stronger contrast. Fabrics for the on point squares should match the central panel to give a more dramatic effect. Match the binding with the strongest colour in the panel, for example black with black or royal blue with royal blue.

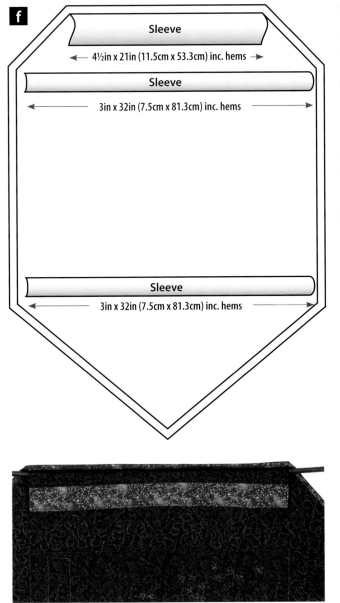

f

Sleeve

◄— 4½in x 21in (11.5cm x 53.3cm) inc. hems —►

Sleeve

◄— 3in x 32in (7.5cm x 81.3cm) inc. hems —►

Sleeve

◄— 3in x 32in (7.5cm x 81.3cm) inc. hems —►

TIP

We recommend a compressed wadding for wallhangings. It has that 'felted' feel and is low loft and needle punched for easy machine or hand quilting. It also stays flat.

Kinkakuji Wallhanging

This beautiful wallhanging will adorn any room in the home. It was originally designed around the Kona Bay limited edition range of fabrics called the Emperor Collection. This particular main panel depicts The Golden Pavilion (Kinkakuji), which was constructed in the late 14th century for the retired shogun, Yoshimitsu.

The wallhanging looks just as pleasing with a larger central panel, framed with two coordinating fabrics in smaller panels, above and below. These fabrics need to complement the main panel in colour and pattern, so choose them with care.

WHAT YOU NEED

- One 24in (60cm) large print design or panel
- Two 20in x 22in (50cm x 56cm) different design oriental prints
- 39¼in (1m) plain black fabric.
- 30in (76cm) Bondaweb
- 35in x 55in (89cm x 140cm) firm wadding (e.g. Thermolam)
- 59in (1.5m) backing fabric

Finished size: 28in x 45in (71cm x 114.3cm) approx.

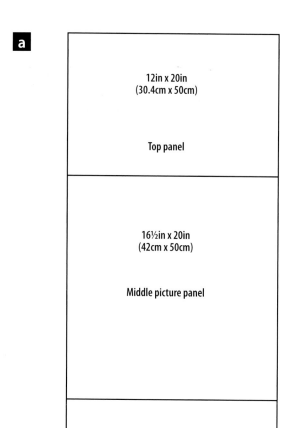

a

12in x 20in
(30.4cm x 50cm)

Top panel

16½in x 20in
(42cm x 50cm)

Middle picture panel

13in x 20in
(33cm x 50cm)

Bottom panel

Construction

1 From the large print/panel and the oriental prints, select the most appropriate areas and cut to the sizes shown in diagram **a**. Try to keep the width of these pieces no less than 20in (50cm) otherwise the dividing strip will not fit. The depth of the panels can alter (the size stated is only a guideline). Sew the chosen panels together using a ¼in (6mm) seam allowance.

2 Cut out the two pattern pieces provided (see templates page 121) for the dividing strips and join as shown in diagram **b**.

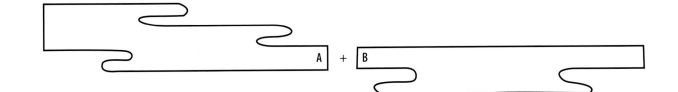

3 Now transfer this shape on to the Bondaweb. Do not forget to reverse the pattern or it will turn out the wrong way. Roughly cut out the Bondaweb shape and iron to the reverse of your black fabric. Cut out the shape, accurately this time. Repeat this shape twice more and, following the dashed lines in the templates on page 121, produce shapes and bonded fabric for the top and bottom strips.

4 Apply these dividing strips across the joins of the pieced panel in the same way as the top and bottom strips (above). See diagram **c**.

TIP

When you use any type of fusible web, always cover your ironing board and the fabric to be bonded with baking parchment or greaseproof paper – this saves getting glue on your iron and board.

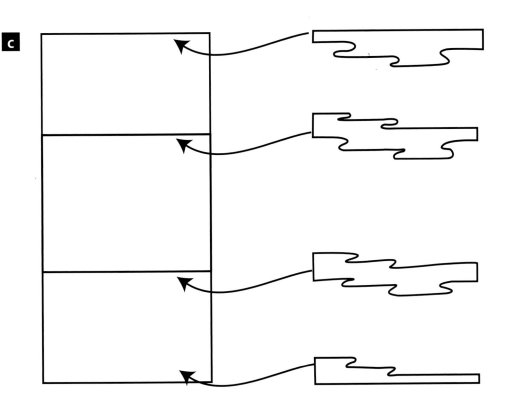

5 You will need to cut strips for borders according to the length of the panel. The side strips should be cut 4½in (11.5cm) wide and the top and bottom strips should be cut 3in (7.5cm) wide. Attach to the main panel in the order shown on diagram **d**. Layer with wadding and backing fabric and tack into place.

6 If you wish, you could cut out various motifs from the remaining pieces of the large design fabric to extend over the borders, as was done with the Wallhangings on page 42.

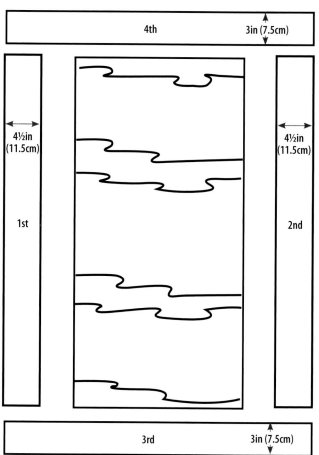

d

4th — 3in (7.5cm)

4½in (11.5cm) — 1st

4½in (11.5cm) — 2nd

3rd — 3in (7.5cm)

7 Neaten the edges of the dividing strips either by hand or by machine. Quilt the panels, again, either by hand or machine. See the templates on pages 122–123 for some quilting design suggestions. We used blossom branches, which are ideal for borders, sakura (cherry blossom) and kaede (maple leaves).

TIP

When neatening the edges of the dividing panels, a machined small satin or zig-zag stitch looks great, but it's worth practising on scraps – some of the curves can be challenging.

$\mathcal{8}$ The edge of the wallhanging needs to be bound and a hanging sleeve added at both the top and bottom edges to accommodate thin battens or canes to ensure it hangs well (see instructions, page 115).

(see instructions, page 115).

TIP

Rayon threads are easy to use by machine and have a lovely sheen. You can use metallic threads but they do have a tendency to snap. There is a huge range of Rayon and other decorative threads available and we have used more than one colour. Some of the leaves are sewn in blue and purple to reflect the colours in the top panel, a gold coloured thread for the sakura branches and appliqué pieces reflects the gold outlining on the fabrics.

FABRIC CHOICE

As the Kinkakuji wallhanging has black as the dominant colour, you are not so tied with the colours in the panels as with the Hokusai wallhanging (page 38) and almost anything goes. Choose boldly, bright coloured patterns with touches of black work really well.

Instead of black, you could try using navy blue or a deep purple for your borders, especially if these colours feature in part of your panels.

Momoyama Holdall

We all appreciate the environmental implications of using too many carrier bags so it is always satisfying to be able to make a multi-use holdall. Whether it's for carrying sewing supplies to class, or for shopping, the handy outside pocket gives quick access to car or door keys. The boxed corners technique saves having to inset side gussets.

'Momoyama' refers to a period in Japanese history in the late 16th century. The autumnal toned fabric that has been used is from the range of the same name by Moda fabrics. The figures depicted are wearing clothes from this period.

WHAT YOU NEED

- 25in x 44in (63.5cm x 112cm) feature fabric
- 30in x 44in (76cm x 112cm) lining fabric
- Selection of fabrics in narrow strips of varying widths
- 20in x 44in (50cm x 112cm) compressed wadding for bag body
- 11in x 19in (27.5cm x 47.5cm) lightweight 2oz wadding for pocket.

Cutting instructions

Feature fabric:

- two 4in x 16in (10cm x 40cm) rectangles for pieced panel
- one 6½in x 16in (16.5cm x 40cm) rectangle for pieced panel
- one 18in x 16in (45cm x 40cm) rectangle for back panel
- one 4in x 24in (10cm x 60cm) strip for handle
- one 18in x 10in (45cm x 25cm) piece for pocket lining
- four 3in (7.5cm) squares for bead ends

Lining fabric:

- two 18in x 16in (45cm x 40cm) rectangles for lining
- two 3in x 16in (7.5cm x 40cm) rectangles for pieced panel
- one 4in x 24in (10cm x 60cm) strip for handle
- one 2½in x 20in (6.3cm x 50cm) strip for pocket binding
- four 2in x 10in (5cm x 25cm) strips for side ties

Compressed wadding:

- two 18in x 16in (45cm x 40cm) rectangles
- two 1½in x 24in (3.8cm x 60cm) strips for handles

Finished size: 16in x 14in x 3in (40.6cm x 35.5cm x 7.6cm) approx.

Making the main panels

Layer the 16in x 18in (40cm x 45cm) feature fabric back panel with wadding and cross hatch quilt at 3in (7.5cm) intervals. Assemble the sections for the pieced panel as in diagram **a**. Layer with wadding and quilt. The dashed lines are suggested quilting lines. Trim any excess wadding.

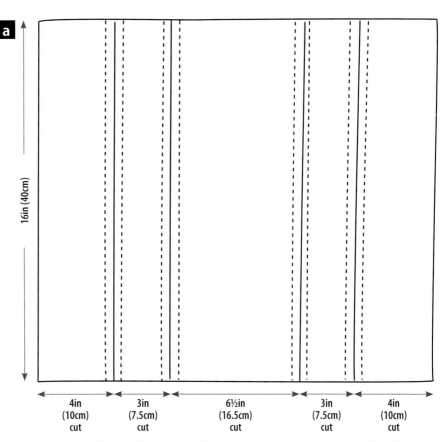

16in (40cm)

| 4in (10cm) cut | 3in (7.5cm) cut | 6½in (16.5cm) cut | 3in (7.5cm) cut | 4in (10cm) cut |

Making the strip-pieced pocket

1 Take a piece of lightweight wadding measuring 19in x 11in (48cm x 28cm) and, using the 'sew and flip' method, cover the wadding in various width strips as shown in diagram **b**. Trim and square up your pieced panel to measure 18in x 10in (45cm x 25cm).

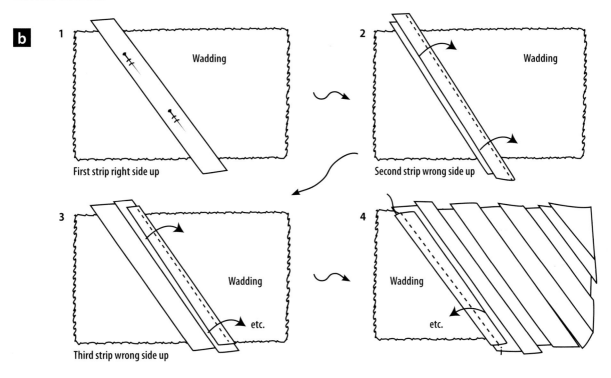

1 First strip right side up
Wadding

2 Second strip wrong side up
Wadding

3 Third strip wrong side up
Wadding
etc.

4 Wadding
etc.

2 Layer your strip-pieced panel with the lining section wrong sides together. Tack all around the outside edge. Fold the 2½in (6.3cm) binding strip in half, lengthways, wrong sides together and use to bind the upper edge of the pocket panel. Tack the pocket to the quilted feature fabric panel and mark vertical lines 6in (15.2cm) in from both edges. Double stitch, starting from the base of the pocket, to create three pocket sections (diagram **c**).

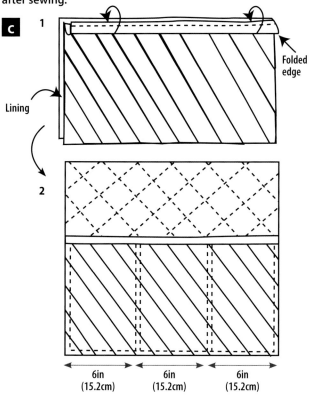

c **1**

Folded edge

Lining

2

6in (15.2cm)   6in (15.2cm)   6in (15.2cm)

Making the handles

1 Using the two 4in x 24in (10cm x 60cm) strips, turn and press a ¼in (6mm) hem along one long edge of each strip. Place a 1½in (3.8cm) strip of wadding along the centre of each strip. Half cover the wadding with the raw edge, then bring over the neatened edge, tack and then sew (diagram **d**). Sew more than one row of stitching – handles look quite good with multiple sewing lines and it also makes the handle stronger and less prone to folding.

d

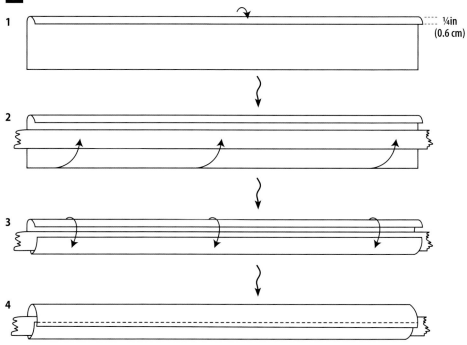

1   ¼in (0.6 cm)

2

3

4

2 Attach the feature fabric handle to the pieced panel of the bag, leaving a 5in (12.5cm) gap between the handle ends. Repeat for the other handle on the pocketed section. Secure in place (see diagram (**e**).

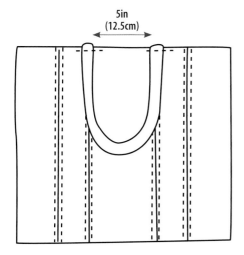

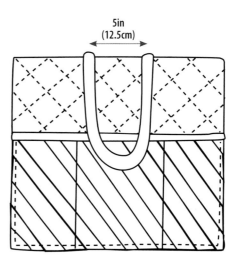

3 Place a piece of lining fabric, right sides together, on to each panel and, using a good ¼in (6mm) seam, sew layers together, where possible reinforcing the seam as you go over the handles (diagram **f**).

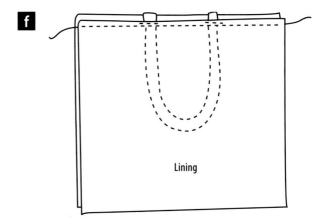

4 Open out and place the two sections together, back and pocket panels facing each other and the two linings likewise. Stitch all layers together as in diagram **g**, using a good ¼in (6mm) seam and leaving a gap for turning in the base of the lining section.

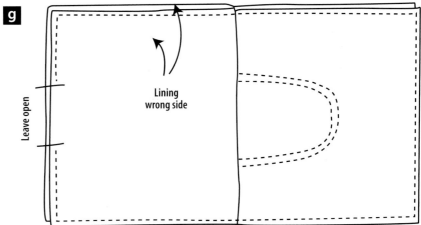

5 Box all the corners as shown (diagram **h**), trim the excess and turn your bag inside out. Slip stitch the opening and push out all the corners. Making sure the lining is well turned in, top stitch through all the layers around the top of the bag.

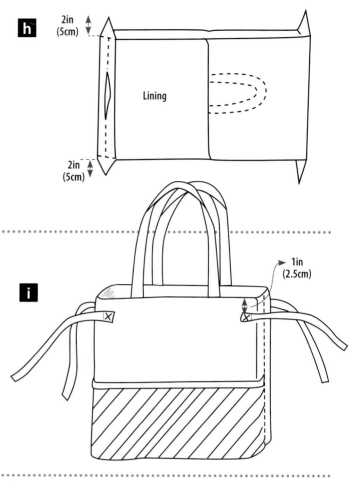

h

2in
(5cm)

Lining

2in
(5cm)

Making the side ties

Fold each 2in x 10in (5cm x 25cm) strip in half lengthways, right sides together. Sew a scant ¼in (6mm) seam along the length; turn tube inside out, press and top stitch. Fold under ½in (1.3cm) of one end on each tie, position on the bag as shown and stitch in place through all layers (see diagram **i**). To make the fabric bead ends, see Yonjuu Sankaku Bag instructions, page 12.

i

1in
(2.5cm)

Finishing the bag

Cover a piece of heavy-duty card, about 5in x 11½in (12.5cm x 29cm) in lining fabric and place in the base of the bag to help keep its shape.

FABRIC CHOICE

Initially find a fabric with a theme as this adds interest to the panels in the main body of the bag. A lot of fabrics are in 'collections' so you can be spoilt for choice. For a coordinate, it's always good fun going through your stash of oddments to find strips for the pieced pocket. It's also an opportunity for you to reacquaint yourself with fabrics from old projects – like revisiting old friends.

Momoyama Purse

This small purse is just big enough to carry two pieces of 'plastic' and some change – you don't always need to take all your worldly goods with you! It is also fairly quick to make so would make an ideal last minute gift for a friend.

WHAT YOU NEED

- 6in x 44in (15.2cm x 112cm) outer feature fabric
- 6in x 44in (15.2cm x 112cm) lining fabric
- 48in (122cm) bias for binding – we have cut our own at 1½in (3.8cm) wide
- Small selection of fabrics in narrow strips in varying widths
- Wadding
- Fabric stabilizer e.g. Vilene
- Magnetic bag closure

Finished size: 4½in x 5½in (11.5cm x 14cm)

Cutting instructions
From feature fabric:
- one 5½in x 4½in (14cm x 11.5cm) piece for purse front
- two 5½in x 3in (14cm x 7.5cm) pieces for credit card section
From lining fabric:
- one 7½in x 5½in (19cm x 14cm) piece for back and flap lining
- one 5½in x 4½in (14cm x 11.5cm) piece for front lining
- four gusset panels (see template section, page 125)

Construction

1 Cut a piece of wadding 6in x 8in (15.2cm x 20cm) and strip piece following the 'sew and flip' method described for the Momoyama Holdall pocket, page 53.

2 Trim to 5½in x 7½in (14cm x 19cm) and curve the top corners as in diagram **a**.

3 Layer the purse front (feature fabric) with wadding and quilt.

4 To make the credit card section, place the two 3in x 5½in (7.5cm x 14cm) rectangles right sides facing and, using a ¼in (6mm) seam, join along the long edge. Turn right sides out, press the seam and top stitch. Attach to the bottom edge of the lining section for the back and flap by stitching through the centre to create two sections. Reinforce the top of this panel with a small piece of Vilene (on the wrong side of the fabric) before attaching the first half of your magnetic closure according to the manufacturer's instructions (see diagram **b**).

5 Attach the other half of the magnetic closure to the front of the quilted front panel as shown in diagram **c**.

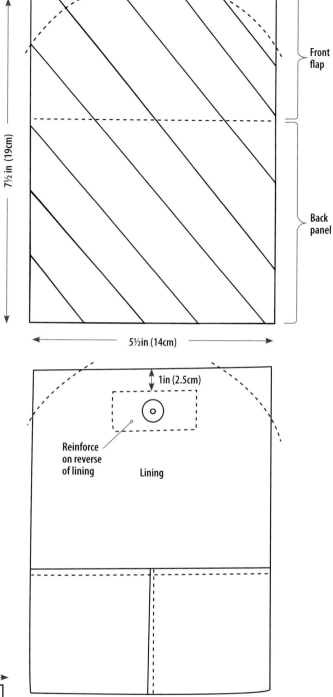

a

Front flap

Back panel

7½ in (19cm)

5½in (14cm)

b

1in (2.5cm)

Reinforce on reverse of lining

Lining

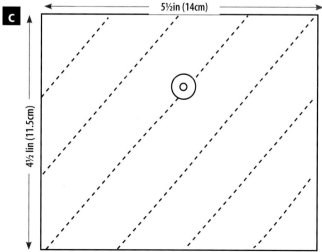

c

5½in (14cm)

4½ in (11.5cm)

6 Apply a piece of Vilene to the reverse of the front panel lining – this will stop the back of the closure from rubbing against the fabric.

7 Tack the lining sections to their relevant outer sections, wrong sides together.

8 Use the template on page 125 to cut four gusset pieces from the lining fabric. Take two of these and place right sides together. Sew together using a ¼in (6mm) seam allowance along the top curved edge. Clip the curves. Turn right sides out, press the curved edge and top stitch. Fold in half along its length, press and top stitch close to the folded edge to give a sharp fold (diagram **d**). Repeat with the other two gusset pieces.

d

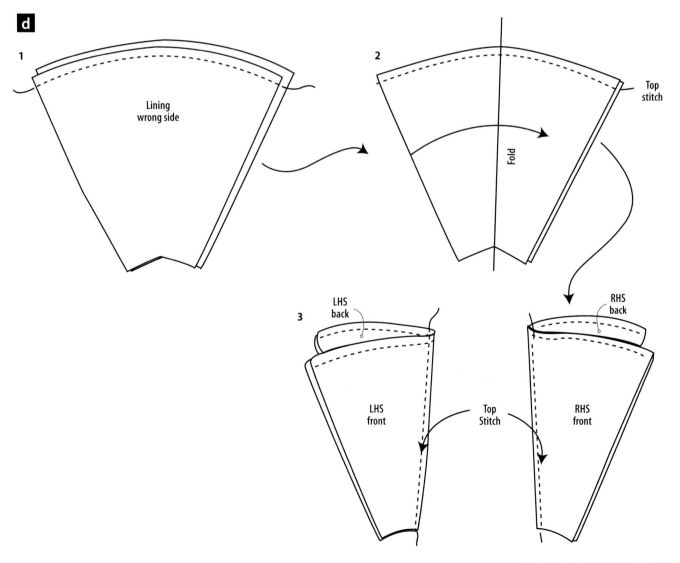

9 Place the folded gussets at the edges of the credit card pocket. Tack the back gusset flaps in place as shown (diagram **e**).

10 Tack the front panel to the front gusset flaps. Then stitch through all the layers to provide a line between the top flap and back sections as shown (diagram **f**).

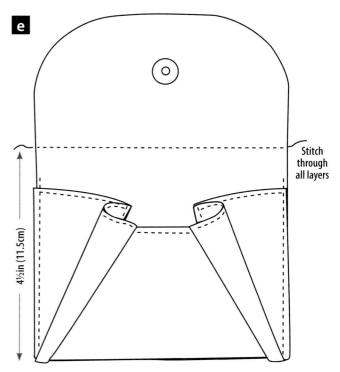

e

Stitch through all layers

4½in (11.5cm)

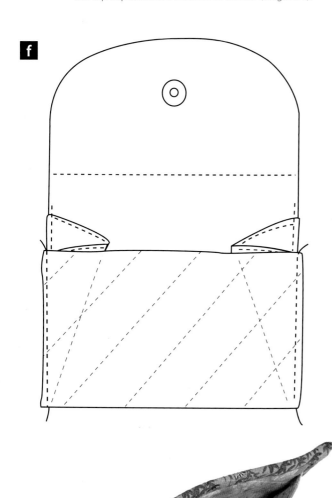

f

11 Bind the back and flap panel, applying the binding from the strip pieced side. Do not bind the lower edge. Bind the front panel on three sides, following general binding instructions on pages 114–115, mitring top corners as you go. Now bind the lower edge, taking in all raw edges of the back and front panels.

Takusan Tsugi Quilt

This richly coloured lap quilt can be made from an organised range of fabrics or, as in this case, from a charm pack, allowing the use of a wider range – hence the name Takusan Tsugi meaning 'many patch'. The narrow black sashing allows for normally clashing colours and designs to sit quite happily together.

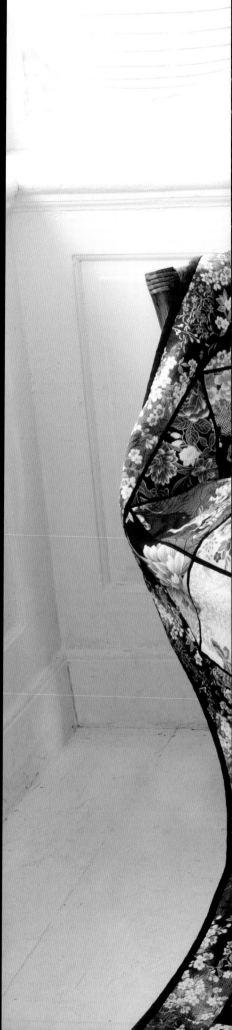

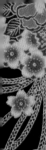

WHAT YOU NEED

- Thirty-nine 6in (15.2cm) squares
- Twenty 6in (15.2cm) squares for triangular insets.
  OR: Seven different fat quarters. Each fat quarter will give
  you nine 6in (15.2cm) squares
- 30in (76cm) plain black fabric for sashing, inner border
  and binding
- 20in (50cm) outer border fabric
- 118in (3m) of ¼in (6mm) black bias binding
- Oddments of fabric and thin wadding for appliqué circles
- Piece of wadding 44in x 60in (112cm x 152cm)
- Backing fabric 44in x 60in (112cm x 152cm)
- Black thread

Cutting instructions

Black fabric:

- cut one 6in x 44in (15.2cm x 112cm)
  strip. Cut this into forty-eight strips
  6in x ¾in (15.2cm x 2cm) for sashing.
- cut eleven ¾in x 44in (2cm x 112cm)
  strips for sashing and inner border and
  five 2½in x 44in (6.3cm x 112cm) strips
  for binding

Outer border fabric:

- cut five 3½in x 44in (9cm x 112cm)
  strips

Squares:

- cut twenty 6in (15.2cm) squares into
  triangles by cutting a good ¼in (6mm)
  beyond the diagonal. Use the larger
  'halves' (diagram **a**)

Finished size: 39in x 54in (99cm x 137cm)

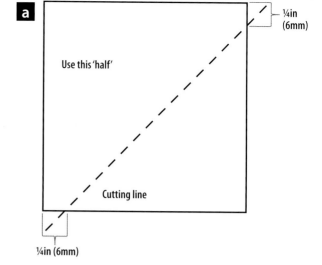

a

Use this 'half'

¼in (6mm)

Cutting line

¼in (6mm)

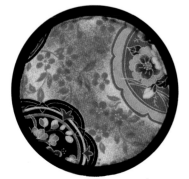

Construction

1 Select and lay out your chosen 39 squares and 20 triangles as shown in diagram **b**.

2 Using a consistent ¼in (6mm) seam, sew a 6in x ¾in (15.2 x 2cm) sashing strip between each triangle and square as shown in diagram **c**. Iron seams towards the squares and triangles.

b

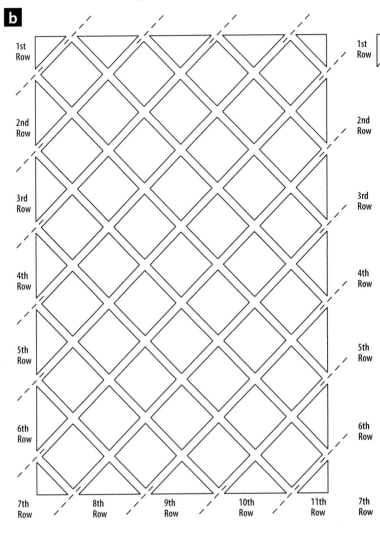

1st Row
2nd Row
3rd Row
4th Row
5th Row
6th Row
7th Row 8th Row 9th Row 10th Row 11th Row

c

1st Row
2nd Row
3rd Row
4th Row
5th Row
6th Row
7th Row 8th Row 9th Row 10th Row 11th Row

TIP

When laying out your squares and triangles, pin your pieces to an old sheet or design wall so that you can stand back to judge that the colour distribution is even.

3 Now sew the rows together using the longer ¼in (6mm) strips, making certain to line up the vertical sashing on each row with the previous row. Iron all seams towards the squares.

4 Trim the quilt top by cutting away any excess edges. Make sure to leave a good ¼in (6mm) seam allowance.

5 As all the edging triangles are cut on the cross and liable to stretch, you will need to stabilize the edge by adding the ¾in (2cm) inner border strips.

Measure across the centre of the quilt top (diagram **d**) and cut two ¾in (2cm) black strips to this size. You will need to join strips to make them long enough. Pin one each to the top and bottom of your patchwork. Make it fit by easing in if necessary. Iron seams towards patchwork. Repeat for the long edges (diagram **e**).

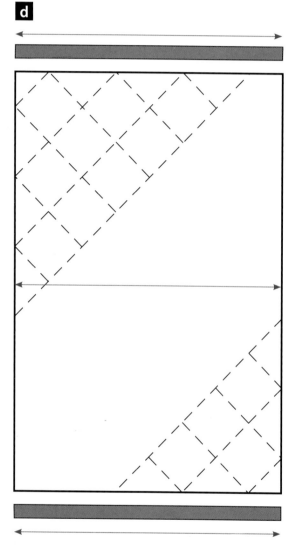

d

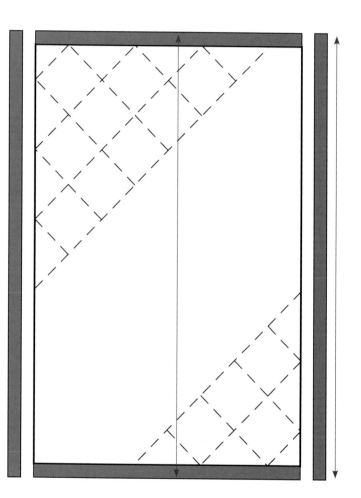

e

6 Repeat this sequence with the outer border. Iron seams towards the outer edges.

7 Layer the quilt with wadding and backing fabric. Tack or pin layers together.

8 Quilt either by hand or machine through the centres of all the sashing strips and inner black border.

9 Bind the edges (see Techniques section, pages 114–115).

TIP

Whenever you add borders to a quilt always measure across the centre of the quilt to establish the true size of the borders to be added. Measuring the side or just sewing on the borders will invariably result in a wavy edge!

Adding decorative circles

Cut seven circles of fabric from oddments in varying sizes (diagram **f**). Cut a slightly smaller corresponding circle out of thin wadding. Tack wadding to fabric. Place each circle on the quilt at a sashing intersection wherever you think they look the most balanced. Tack in place. Edge each circle with ¼in (6mm) black bias tape. Turn the end to neaten and sew in place either by hand or machine.

TIP

The placement of your circles may well be determined by how well your sashing strips line up – if some are a bit 'out', the choice is already made.

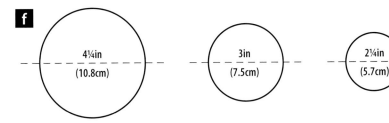

f
- 4¼in (10.8cm)
- 3in (7.5cm)
- 2¼in (5.7cm)

FABRIC CHOICE

Be bold with your colour and design choices with this project. Even very large prints can be 'fussy cut' to produce many different aspects from the same fabric. Cut your own 6in (15.2cm) squares from fabric in your stash – you may be surprised at how many you have. The main appeal of this quilt is the random nature of the square placement, but you could limit your palette to a narrow range of colours – try blacks, reds and golds for a very rich and regal look.

The border fabric needs careful consideration; it helps to tie the whole project together if you use some of the border fabric as edging triangles to the pieced panel.

Takusan Tsugi Cushion

Whenever you make a quilt there are always leftovers. This cushion makes a great partner to the Takusan Tsugi Quilt (page 62) and will make good use of some of the odds and ends. The envelope backs are lined to make the entire cushion cover more substantial.

WHAT YOU NEED

- Five 5½in (14cm) squares
- Eight triangles. These are the smaller 'halves' leftover from the Takusan Tsugi quilt or four 6½in (16.5cm) squares cut in half diagonally
- 12in x 44in (30.4 x 112cm) black fabric for sashing and binding
- 20in x 44in (50cm x 112cm) border/backing fabric
- 14in x 44in (35.5cm x 112cm) lining fabric (to line envelope backs)
- One 20in (50cm) square of wadding and butter muslin
- Two 3in (7.5cm) circles
- Two 2½in (6.3cm) circles
- 39¼in x ¼in (1m x 6mm) black bias
- 18in–20in (45cm–50cm) cushion pad

Cutting instructions

From black fabric:
- ten 5½in x ¾in (14cm x 2cm) strips
- three 44in x ¾in (112cm x 2cm) strips
- one 44in x 1½in (112cm x 3.8cm) strip
- two 44in x 2½in (112cm x 6.3cm) strips for binding

From border/backing fabric:
- two 2¼in x 16in (5.7cm x 40cm) strips
- two 2¼in x 19in (5.7cm x 48cm) strips
- one 20in x 12½in (50cm x 31.7cm) backing piece (lower section)
- one 20in x 7¾in (50cm x 19.7cm) backing piece (upper section)
- one 20in x 3½in (50cm x 9cm) backing piece (upper section)

From lining fabric:
- two 13in x 21in (33cm x 53.3cm) rectangles

Finished size: 19in x 19in (48cm x 48cm) approx.

Construction

1 Select and lay out your chosen five squares and eight triangles as in diagram **a**.

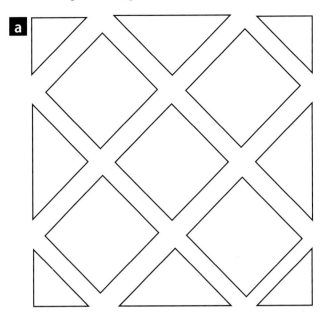

2 Using a consistent ¼in (6mm) seam, sew a 5½in x ¾in (14cm x 2cm) sashing strip between each triangle and square as in diagram **b**. Iron seams towards the squares and triangles.

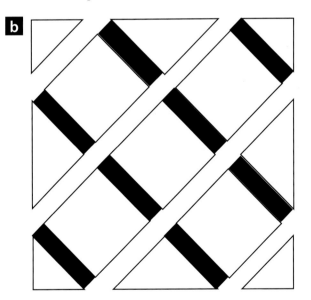

3 Now sew the rows together using the longer ¾in (2cm) strips, making certain to line up the vertical sashing on each row with the previous row. Iron all seams towards the squares.

4 Square up your panel – it should measure 15in (38cm) square. This allows a good ¼in (6mm) beyond the points (see diagram **c**).

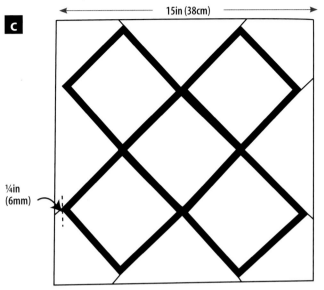

5 Add a ¾in (2cm) strip to all four sides, taking care not to stretch your panel out of shape – the edging triangles are cut on the cross and stretch easily. Iron seams towards the patchwork. Add your 2¼in (5.7cm) border strips – firstly to the top and bottom of the panel – ironing seams outwards and then the strips to the two sides (diagram **d**).

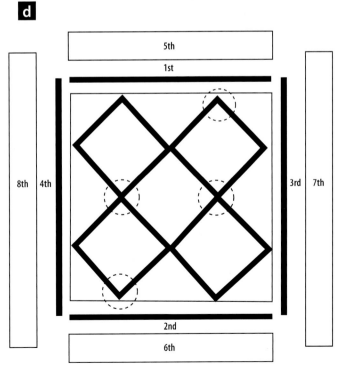

6 Layer your panel with wadding and muslin, tack and quilt. Apply circles to your quilted top in the same manner as for the Takusan Tsugi Quilt (page 67).

Making envelope backs

1 To make the envelope backs for your cushion cover, piece the upper section as shown in diagram **e**.

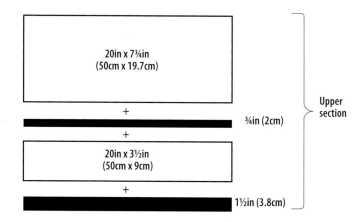

e

20in x 12½in
(50cm x 31.7cm)

Lower section

20in x 7¾in
(50cm x 19.7cm)

+

¾in (2cm)

+

20in x 3½in
(50cm x 9cm)

+

1½in (3.8cm)

Upper section

2 With right sides facing, layer each backing section with a piece of lining fabric. Seam together along one long edge as indicated in diagram **f**.

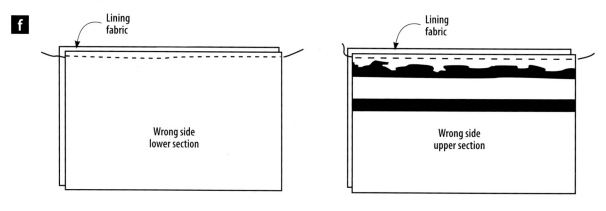

f

Lining fabric

Wrong side lower section

Lining fabric

Wrong side upper section

3 Fold each lining piece back, press and top stitch along the folded edge. Trim the edges to the same width as your cushion cover top.

4 With wrong sides facing, layer the envelope backs on to the reverse of your cushion top (diagram **g**). Tack in place.

g

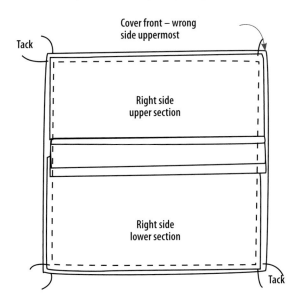

Cover front – wrong side uppermost

Tack

Right side upper section

Right side lower section

Tack

5 Bind the edges following the binding instructions on pages 114–115.

When using a fabric with a directional design, make sure that the panels are all running the same way. The black binding reflects the sashing on the cushion front.

Shoji Screen Wallhanging

This wallhanging is based on a 'shoji' screen using four individual, stylised panels. These are all simply made using fusible web with a satin stitch finish. The appliqué is created using marble effect and small print Oriental style fabrics. The background colours represent the translucent materials used in shoji screen design.

WHAT YOU NEED

- Noshi (ribbons) and fans: four or five Oriental style prints, each 6in x 22in (15.2cm x 56cm)
- Tree and irises: three green, two brown, one or two purples, each 6in x 22in (15.2cm x 56cm)
- Screen background: 44in x 22in (112cm x 56cm)
- Final background and binding: 44in x 47in (112cm x 120cm)
- Black binding: 44in x 10in (112cm x 25cm)
- Backing: 44in x 47in (112cm x 120cm)
- Wadding for screens and backing: 44in x 69in (112cm x 175cm)
- Fusible web: 17in x 20in (43cm x 50cm)
- Black ribbon: ⅛in x 390in (3mm x 10m)
- Gold ribbon: ⅛in x 20in (3mm x 50cm)
- Sleeve fabric: 5in x 44in (12.5cm x 112cm)
- Threads: gold, green, brown, purple and/or monofilament (optional)

Finished size: 44in x 22in (112cm x 56cm) approx.

TIP

Take time to experiment with the position of the appliqués to achieve a balanced and harmonious look. Avoid placing them too centrally.

Construction

1 Using the templates on page 124, trace all the patterns on to fusible web. Cut out the patterns and fuse to the wrong side of your chosen fabrics.

2 Take your background fabric and cut four pieces, each 21in x 10½in (53.3cm x 26.7cm). Cut an angle at the top and bottom of each piece (see diagram **a**).

a

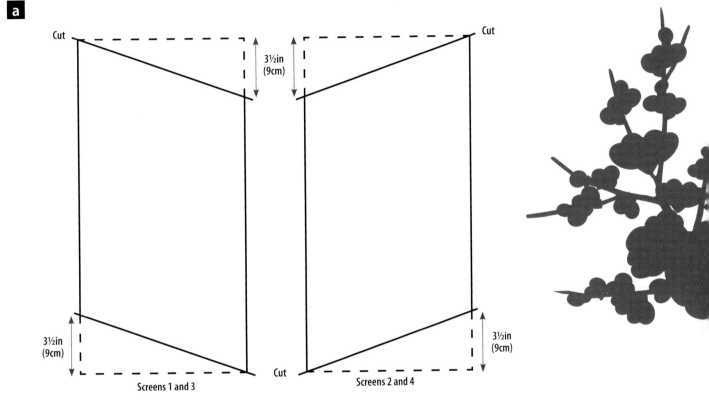

Cut

Cut

3½in (9cm)

3½in (9cm)

3½in (9cm)

Cut

Screens 1 and 3

Screens 2 and 4

3 Place all fabrics – tree, noshi, fans and irises – in position on the screen pieces. When you are satisfied with the positioning, press into place.

TIP

To hang the screen over a bed or behind a sofa, either fit a sleeve top and bottom (fit a baton in the bottom sleeve to give it weight) or tab the top with about five tabs, placed evenly. You can then fix the hanging with a metal pole with scrolled ends or a wooden pole. See the instructions for making sleeves and tab tops on page 115.

4 Cut four pieces of wadding exactly the same size as the screens. Layer with the screen pieces and tack together. Take each screen and satin stitch all edges of the tree, noshi, fans and irises until complete. Place looped gold ribbon, cut approx. 5in (12.5cm), over noshi and stitch down.

TIP

For satin stitching, set your machine to zig-zag, alter your stitch width to 3.5 and length to between 0.3 and 0.4 (if this is possible). It is always advisable to do a test run until you get the desired stitch. Rayon threads make good satin stitch as does long staple Egyptian cotton and there are some beautiful variegated threads on the market now. If you are not too confident with coloured threads, monofilament thread will do just as well, in which case only use a fine zig-zag with a width of 3 to 4 and length not less than 1.

5 Measure the black ribbon from top to bottom of each screen, allowing approx. 1in (2.5cm) beyond the screen measurement. Cut three pieces for each screen and straight stitch them in place. Do the same with the horizontal ribbons until all four are completed (see diagram **b**). Trim excess ribbon.

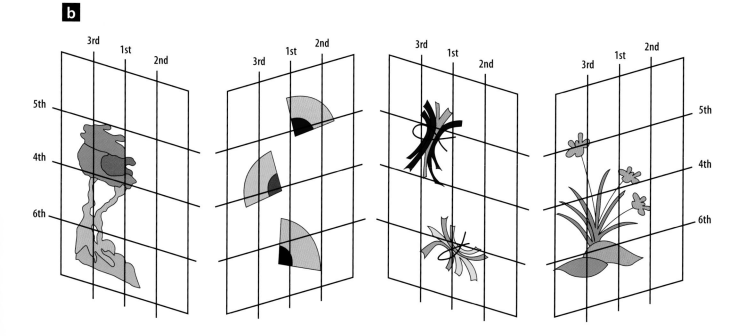

b

6 From the black fabric, cut 1½in (3.8cm) strips from the width of fabric. Join the strips together until you have the required length for each screen. Now sew these strips to the edges of your screens. Mitre the corners following binding instructions on page 114, being aware of the slightly odd angles at the corners. Fold over to the back and press into place, then tack these down with the raw edge facing inwards.

7 Now take your final background fabric, wadding and backing, cut to 47in x 27in (120cm x 67.5cm), layer all the pieces together and tack firmly.

8 Take the four screens and place them on to the final background, measuring as you go, until all four sit evenly (see diagram **c**). Either pin or tack these into position. Here you have a choice for attaching the screens – either hand slip stitch on to the background or blind hem machine on the very edge of the binding. This gives a raised effect and makes the screens stand out.

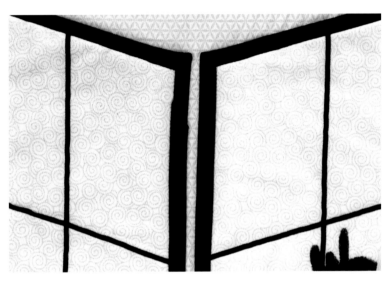

c

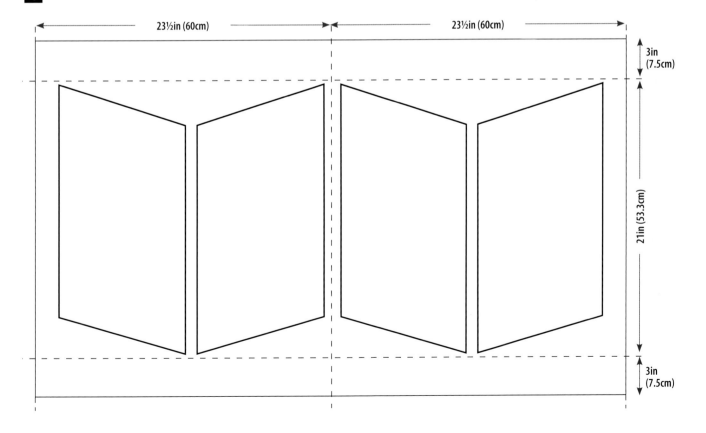

23½in (60cm)   23½in (60cm)

3in (7.5cm)

21in (53.3cm)

3in (7.5cm)

9 Cut your sleeve fabric 5in x 42in (12.5cm x 106.6cm). Turn down one long edge approx ½in (1.3cm) and stitch down. Pin the long raw edge of the sleeve to the top raw edge of your backing fabric, placing it evenly, and tack into place.

10 Cut your final binding from the remainder of the background fabric 2½in x 150in (6.3cm x 3.8m). Sew on to edge of the final background, turn over and slip stitch into place.

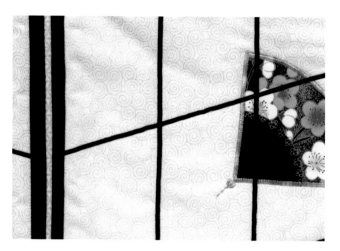

APPLIQUÉ MOTIF CHOICES

We have made our choices for the appliqué motifs based on their significance in Japanese culture. There are many Oriental patterns available, for instance you may like to choose dragons, a geisha, cranes, pine trees or koi – the possibilities are endless.

Some Japanese names, definitions and meanings are as follows:

- Iris – 'hanasyoubu', meaning noble heart.

- Chrysanthemum – 'kiku', meaning elegant or elegance and also the national flower of Japan.

- Dragonfly – signifies love.

- Dragons – many forms appear in Japanese myths and culture. They can signify fertility, humility and a warding off of evil spirits

- Ribbons – 'noshi', signify an auspicious or happy occasion.

- Cherry blossom – 'sakura', an unofficial national flower.

Tobi Ishi Quilted Throw

This quick and easy throw will sit beautifully on a bed or sofa. It is backed with Polar fleece, which makes it lovely and cosy for those long winter evenings.

Tobi ishi means stepping stones and here the charcoal coloured blocks depict the stepping stones in a traditional Japanese garden with the greens, golds and creams adding the other dimensions of shrubs, gravel and sand.

The blocks have been calculated to allow extra for cushions, if desired, and there are instructions for these included on page 88. They are simple to make and add that extra sense of luxury to a bed or sofa.

WHAT YOU NEED

For throw and four cushions, including backing and bindings:

- 12in (30.4cm) patterned cream fabric
- 12in (30.4cm) first and second patterned green fabric
- 12in (30.4cm) first and second patterned gold fabric
- 12in (30.4cm) first and second patterned charcoal fabric
- 78in (2m) plain cream fabric
- 78in (2m) plain green fabric
- 20in (50cm) plain gold fabric
- 39¼in (1m) plain charcoal fabric

Cutting instructions

- Eight 6in (15.2cm) squares of patterned cream
- Eight 6in (15.2cm) squares of first patterned green
- Six 6in (15.2cm) squares of second patterned green
- Six 6in (15.2cm) squares of first and second patterned gold
- Eight 6in (15.2cm) squares of first and second patterned charcoal
- Sixteen 6in x 2in (15.2cm x 5cm) and sixteen 9½in x 2in (24.1cm x 5cm) plain cream rectangles
- Twenty-eight 6in x 2in (15.2cm x 5cm) and twenty-eight 9½in x 2in (24.1cm x 5cm) plain green rectangles
- Twenty-four 6in x 2in (15.2cm x 5cm) and twenty-four 9½in x 2in (24.1cm x 5cm) plain gold rectangles
- Thirty-two 6in x 2in (15.2cm x 5cm) and thirty-two 9½in x 2in (24.1cm x 5cm) plain charcoal rectangles
- Ten 10¾in (27.3cm) plain cream squares
- One 11¾in (29.8cm) plain cream square
- Six 3in x 44in (7.5cm x 112cm) plain cream for outer borders
- Six 1½in x 44in (3.8cm x 112cm) plain charcoal for bindings

Finished size: 80in x 56in (203cm x 142cm)

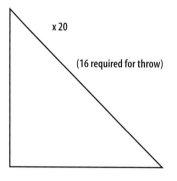

Construction

1 Cut the ten 10¾in (27.3cm) plain cream squares in half diagonally (see diagram **a**). You will need 16 triangles for the throw, set aside four of the triangles for the smaller cushion on page 89.

a

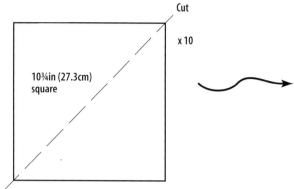

Cut

1

10¾in (27.3cm) square

x 10

2

x 20

(16 required for throw)

2 Cut the 11¾in (29.8cm) plain cream square into four on the diagonal (see diagram **b**). Set these aside for the corners of the throw.

b

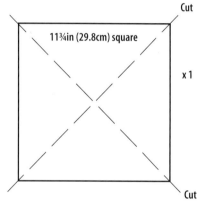

Cut

1

11¾in (29.8cm) square

x 1

Cut

2

x 4

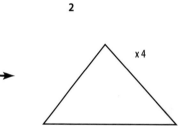

FABRIC CHOICE

The muted colours for this throw were chosen as an alternative to the rich colourings of the Oriental fabrics to give it a more neutral look that will sit happily with many decorative tastes and will look especially good with natural materials like wood and leather. It should also appeal to the men in the household!

The fabrics used, although not Japanese wovens, are of a similar weight and have a more open weave than normal cotton fabrics. The wovens are ideal for sashiko stitching because of this open weave. You can now get a large range of colours in these fabrics and they would make an excellent alternative for this project.

3 Sew matching borders to all squares, cream to cream, green to green etc. (see diagram **c**). Press and square all blocks so that they measure 9in (22.8cm) square. Set aside the following blocks for cushions: two first green, two second green, two first charcoal, four second charcoal.

4 Working on the diagonal (see diagram **d**) follow the pattern to join blocks into rows until all rows are completed. Press the rows and add the triangles to the ends, as shown.

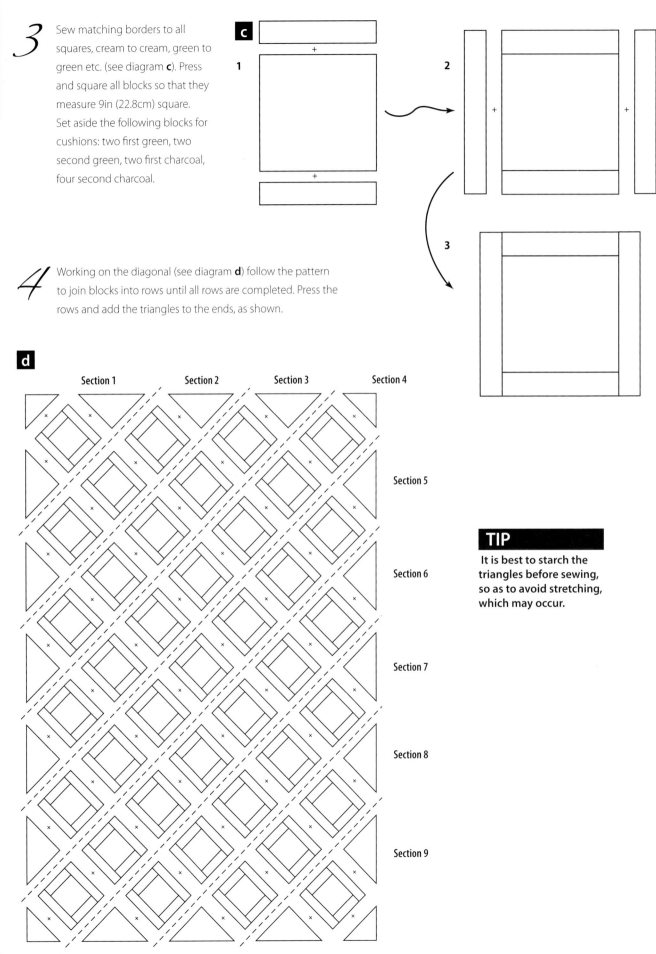

c

d

Section 1   Section 2   Section 3   Section 4

Section 5

Section 6

Section 7

Section 8

Section 9

TIP

It is best to starch the triangles before sewing, so as to avoid stretching, which may occur.

5 Once all the triangles have been added, join the rows together until all nine rows are completed. The four smaller triangles are for the four corners; you may add these at the beginning or when the rows have been sewn together. Level up all edges leaving approx 1½in–2in (3.8cm–5cm) beyond the points.

6 Before adding the outer borders, measure through the centre width and length of the throw top. Measure the border pieces exactly and make them fit into the edges (see diagram **e**). Pin at the ends first and work your way into the middle, easing as you go.

e

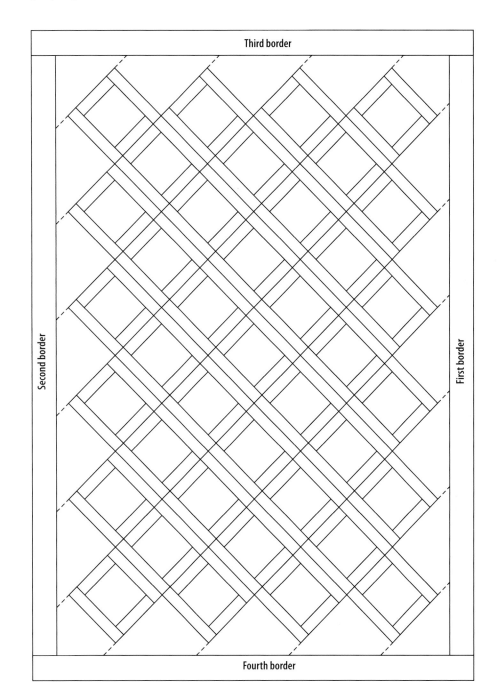

Third border

Second border

First border

Fourth border

7   Give the quilt top a final gentle press and layer with Polar fleece. Here you can either tack together or use a temporary adhesive such as 505 spray, which will hold the layers together during quilting. It is always a good idea to tack the edges even if you use the adhesive.

8   The quilting lines are a simple tramline effect, which you extend approx. ½in (1.3cm) beyond the blocks to form a square.

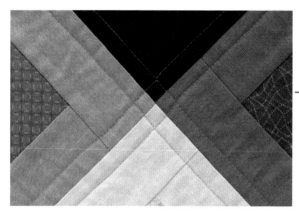

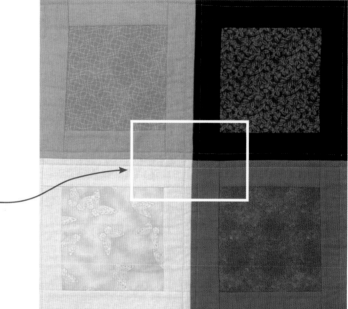

9   Join all the binding strips together. Trim off the corners, press one end down to form a triangle and stitch to the edge of the throw. Finish off in the usual way (see instructions for binding on pages 114–115).

Tobi Ishi Cushions

Once you have made the throw, you can quickly make up cushions with the blocks you have left over. There will be enough to make four cushions, two measuring 18in (45.7cm) square and the other two 13in (33cm) square.

Construction

Larger cushions

1 Join one green block to the left hand side of one charcoal block. Join one charcoal block to the left hand side of one green block. Press the seams and join these together to form a square (see diagram **a**). Repeat to make the second 18in (45.7cm) cushion.

2 Layer the two cushion fronts with wadding and backing (muslin or calico will work equally well). Quilt as desired.

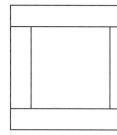

3 Measure and cut eight 18in x 12in (45.7cm x 30.4cm) pieces. Sew two pieces together along the 18in (45.7cm) width, fold along the seam, press and top stitch. Repeat this instruction three more times. Pin these sections to the two backs of the cushions and tack into place (see diagram **b**). Cut four binding strips and bind cushions, following the instructions for binding on pages 114–115.

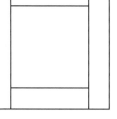
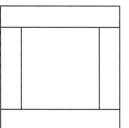
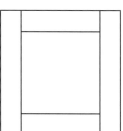

Top stitching

Smaller cushions

1 Take the four triangles you have remaining from the 10¾in (27.3cm) cream squares (see Tobi Ishi Quilted Throw step 1 page 83) and cut them in half diagonally to give you eight smaller triangles. Take one remaining charcoal block and add four of the small triangles. Press the seams. Repeat with the second remaining charcoal block and four small triangles to make the second cushion (see diagram **c**).

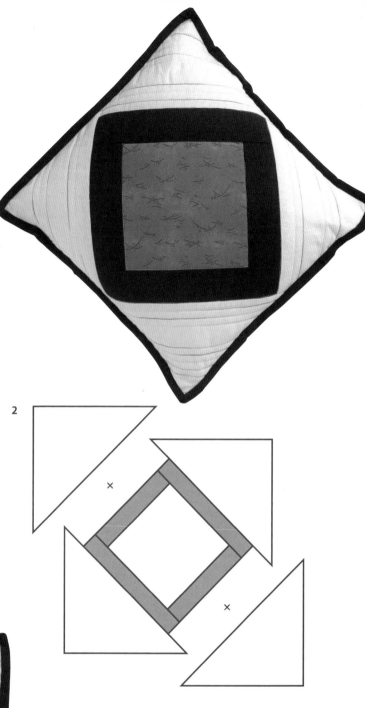

c

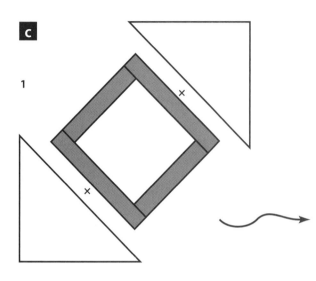

2 Layer the two cushion fronts with wadding and backing. Quilt as desired.

3 Follow the instructions in step 3 of the larger cushion but changing the measurement of the pieces you cut to eight 13in x 6in (33cm x 15.2cm) pieces.

These cushions are so quick and easy to make up with the 'leftovers' from the throw and are a really stylish addition.

Tsukiyama Bed Quilt

'Tsukiyama', which translates to 'strolling garden', is the name chosen for this delightful bed quilt. The blocks with flowers and vibrant colours are akin to flower beds while the green sashing becomes the paths that meander around the garden.

This is an easily pieced quilt, which incorporates those large patterned prints and also combines the beautiful small print fabrics. You can use fabrics that don't necessarily match in colour, although it is important that you choose a fabric for your sashing that will bring all the blocks together.

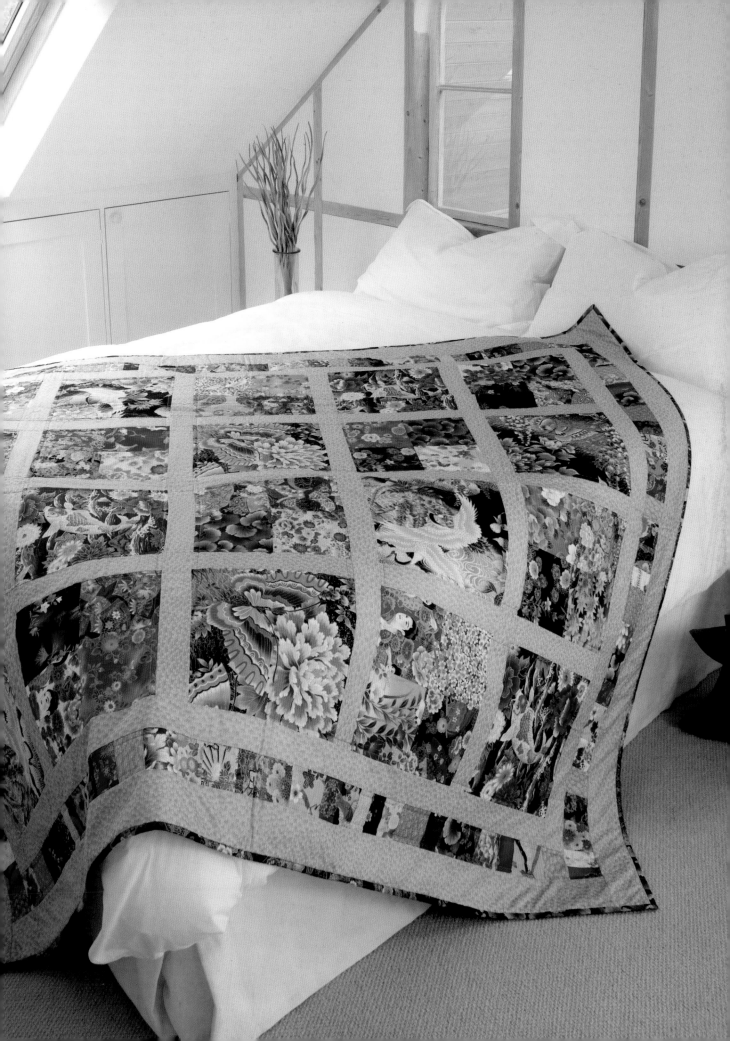

WHAT YOU NEED

- 60in (152.5cm) large print fabric
- Six fat quarters or forty 6in (15.2cm) squares of small print fabric
- 72in (183cm) sashing fabric
- 144in (3.6m) backing fabric, based on 44in (112cm) wide
- 72in (183cm) wadding
- 20in (50cm) binding (this can be the same colour as your sashing fabric)
- The inner border is made up of scraps approximately 1½in to 2½in (3.8cm–6.3cm) wide. You can use the remains of your fat quarters for this border

Cutting instructions

Large blocks:
- ten 11½in x 11½in (29cm x 29cm) squares

Pieced blocks:
- forty 6in x 6in (15.2cm x 15.2cm) squares

Sashing:
- twenty 11½in x 2½ (29cm x 6.3cm) strips
- twenty 13½in x 2½in (34.2cm x 6.3cm) strips
- one 65in x 2½in (165cm x 6.3cm) strip
- one 54in x 2½in (137cm x 6.3cm) strip

Inner border:
- two 54in x 2½in (137cm x 6.3cm) pieced strips
- two 67in x 2½in (170cm x 6.3cm) pieced strips

Outer border:
- two 71in x 3½in (180.5cm x 9cm) strips
- two 64in x 3½in (162cm x 9cm) strips

Binding:
- eight 44in x 2½in (112cm x 6.3cm) strips

Finished size: 77in x 64in (196cm x 163cm) approx.

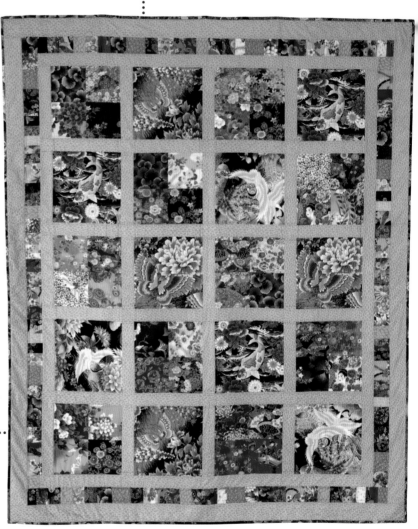

Construction

1 Take your 40 squares and put them into random piles of four until you have ten piles. With a ¼in (6mm) seam allowance, sew four squares together, one from each pile, until you have ten completed blocks (see diagram **a**). Press these.

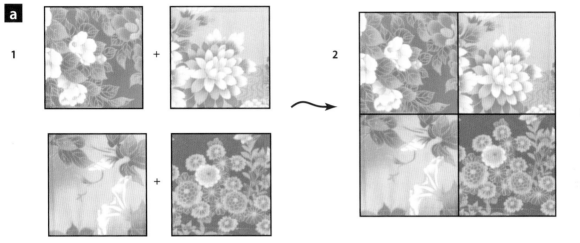

2 Take your sashing fabric and sew the 11½in (29cm) strips to the left side of these blocks and the ten 11½in x 11½in (29cm x 29cm) squares. Press seams. Now take your 13½in (34.2cm) strips and sew them to the to the bottom edge of all your blocks and press the seams (see diagram **b**).

3 Starting from row 1, lay the blocks out, putting them as a pieced block then large block and so-on, four blocks across and five down (see diagram **c**). Don't forget to alternate your blocks, so if you start the first row with a pieced block the second row must start with a large patterned block. Join the blocks together in their rows, making sure that all your sashing pieces fit exactly. Press all five rows.

c

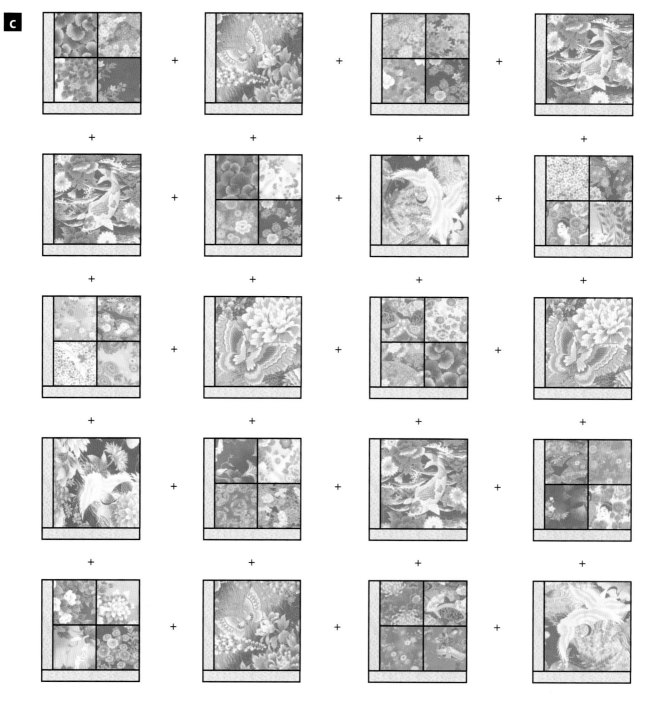

4 Now sew all your rows together pressing each sewn seam as you go (this makes for a crisper finish).

5   Take your remaining sashing and sew it to the right side of
    your rows and then add the top sashing. Remember to
    measure through the centre width and length of your quilt top
    to get the exact size for the sashing strips (see diagram **d**).

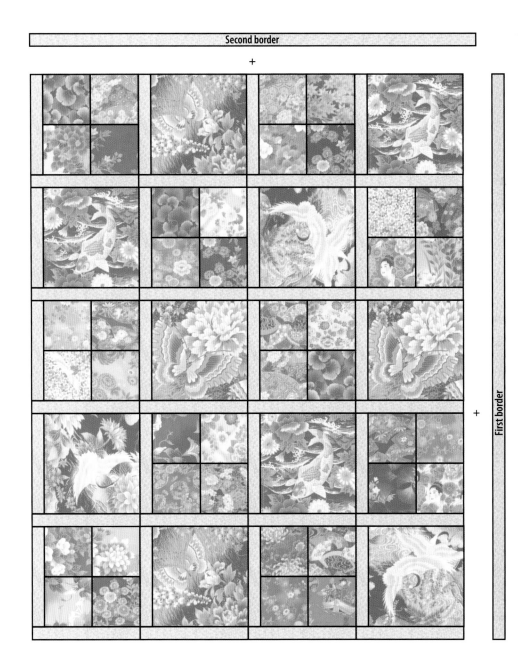

Adding the inner border

1 The pieced inner border is made up of several 6½in (16.5cm) strips. these strips can be scraps or you can use the remainder of your fabrics used within the blocks, any size from 1½in to 2½in (3.8cm to 6.3cm) will be fine. Measure the width and length of your rows – you should have 54in x 67in (137cm x 170cm). Sew the strips in two separate rows, one 54in (137cm) long and one 67in (170cm) long. Press the seams as you join the strips.

2 Once you have the desired lengths, trim the edges and cut 2½in (6.3cm) strips (see diagram **e**).

3 Starting from the lengths, sew the pieced strips (once again pressing the seams), then add the top and bottom borders. Give a final press.

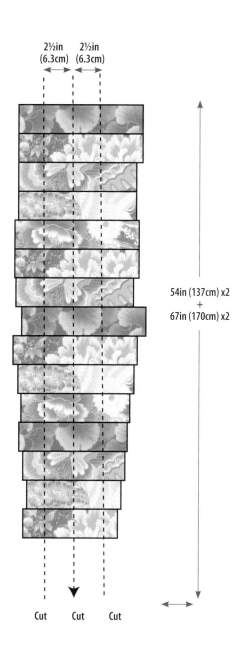

2½in (6.3cm)   2½in (6.3cm)

e

54in (137cm) x2
+
67in (170cm) x2

Cut   Cut   Cut

Adding the outer border

Finally you are ready to add the outer border. Once again, check your measurements. You can ensure the correct fit if you measure the required length on the border fabric, put a pin in exactly that length and make the border fit into the quilt top. Add the lengths first and then the top and bottom, not forgetting to press your seams as you go (see diagram **f**).

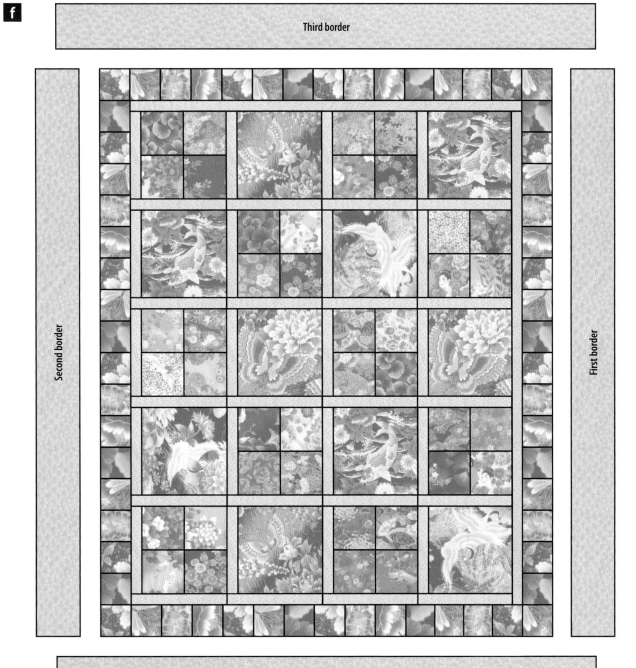

Finishing the quilt

The top is now ready for layering with wadding and backing – a popular alternative is Polar fleece, which is easy to use and warm as well. You can quilt in any pattern you desire. The quilt pictured has a simple tramline effect, which is quick and easy to do, with a contrasting thread and with the walking foot on the sewing machine. With the edge of the foot against the seam, run a straight stitch through all the blocks in both directions.

Finally, add your binding to complete the quilt following the binding instructions on pages 114–115.

TIP

If you do not have a walking foot, release the foot pressure on your machine slightly.

FABRIC CHOICE

We used green sashing to represent the paths around the garden but you can choose a colour that would compliment your bedroom. Because the main fabrics are so vibrant, any blender type fabric will be suitable.

If your room is predominantly pale blue then why not use blue sashing to represent a water garden? We find that plain fabric is too stark so would advise a tone on tone and if it has gold incorporated into it you are adding a bit of sparkle.

TIP

When quilting, especially if using a machine, be careful going across the downward quilting as the fabric has a tendency to start to pucker. Try to ease the fabric towards the foot in between the quilting. This will give you a chance to keep the fabric nice and even.

Geisha Doll

This lovely little doll, originally designed by Julia, has been one of our most popular patterns. It is now transformed by piecing the kimono, which has been adapted from Jenni Dobson's book *'Making Kimono and Japanese Clothes'*. Any little girl would love one of these as a gift; in fact it would make a beautiful gift for a big girl too!

We have produced two alternatives for the kimono. Kimono one is block pieced and we have used Kamon style fabric (kamon means 'family crest'), while kimono two is strip pieced. The fabric requirements overleaf cover both kimono and are set out as two separate cutting instructions as well.

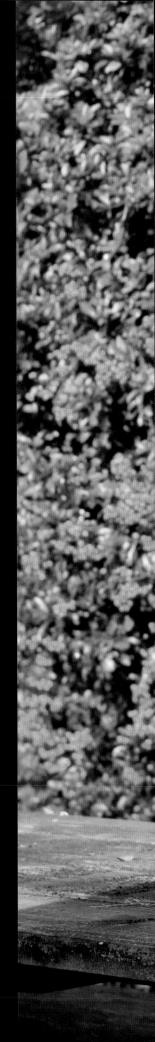

WHAT YOU NEED

For doll:

- 10in x 44in (25cm x 112cm) very pale plain pink fabric
- one bag of toy stuffing
- 6in (15.2cm) wooden dowel or chopstick
- 4in x 20in (10cm x 50cm) plain black fabric

For headdress:

- small silk flowers (available from a good florist) held together with florist wire or fine beading wire
- cocktail sticks with one sharp end cut off and filed down for the chopstick effect

For undergarment 'juban':

- 12in x 44in (30.4cm x 112cm) plain white fabric
- kimono lining 20in x 44in (50cm x 112cm) plain fabric matching the kimono you decide to make

For kimono one:

- 10in x 44in (25cm x 112cm) Kamon style fabric 1
- 20in x 44in (50cm x 112cm) accent fabric

For kimono two:

- 8in x 44in (20cm x 112cm) fabric one
- 12in x 44in (30.4cm x 112cm) fabric two
- 5in x 44in (12.5cm x 112cm) fabric three
- 2in x 44in (5cm x 112cm) fabric four

For belt 'obi':

- 5in x 44in (12.5cm x 112cm) silk fabric and/or contrasting lining
- 20in (50cm) contrasting cord or ribbon
- 1¾in x 6in (4.5cm x 15.2cm) pelmet Vilene

Finished size: 18in (46cm) approx.

Cutting instructions

Kimono one (block pieced):

kamon style fabric:

- one 6in x 6in (15.2cm x 15.2cm) for kimono back
- two 3¾in x 8¼in (9.5cm x 21cm) for kimono sleeves
- two 1½in x 16in (3.8cm x 40cm) for kimono front

accent fabric:

- two 1¼in x 16in (3.2cm x 40cm) for kimono sleeves
- two 3¾in x 8¼in (9.5cm x 21cm) for kimono sleeves
- two 5in x 16in (12.5 x 40cm) for kimono front
- two 1¼in x 16in (3.2cm x 40cm) for kimono back
- one 2in x 6in (5cm x 15.2cm) for kimono back
- one 6in x 9in (15.2cm x 23cm) for kimono back
- one 2in x 14½in (5cm x 37cm) for kimono collar

Kimono two (strip pieced):

fabric one:
- one 6½in x 16in (16.5cm x 40cm) for kimono back
- two 3in x 16in (7.5cm x 40cm) for kimono front

fabric two:
- two 1in x 16in (2.5cm x 40cm) for kimono back
- two 1½in x 16in (3.8cm x 40cm) for kimono front
- two 1¾in x 16in (4.4cm x 40cm) for kimono sleeves
- one 2in x 14½in (5cm x 37cm) for kimono collar

fabric three:
- two 2½in x 16in (6.3cm x 40cm) for kimono front
- two 1¾in x 16in (4.5cm x 40cm) for kimono sleeves

fabric four:
- two 2in x 16in (5cm x 40cm) for kimono sleeves

Lining, undergarment and hair:

kimono lining:
- one 7½in x 16in (19cm x 40cm) for lining back
- two 6in x 16in (15.2cm x 40cm) for lining front
- two 4½in x 16in (11.5cm x 40cm) for lining sleeves

undergarment 'juban':
- one 7½in x 15½in (19cm x 39.4cm) for juban back
- two 5in x 15½in (12.5cm x 39.4cm) for juban front
- one 2in x 9in (5cm x 23cm) for juban collar

black fabric for hair:
- one 4in x 12in (10cm x 30.4cm) and a 4in (10cm) circle

Construction

1 From the templates on page 125, either trace or cut out the body patterns. Referring to diagram **a**, lay these on to double thickness doll fabric and draw around the shapes leaving a ¼in (6mm) seam allowance around all pieces. Machine stitch around the drawn lines using a small stitch. Cut out the body and arms, clip all the curves and turn right side out. Turn under a ¼in (6mm) at the bottom edge of the body and tack.

2 Take the toy stuffing and fill the head, adding the dowel/ chopstick before continuing around the neck area and down the body, shaping into place as you go. Using the 4in (10cm) circle template on page 125, cut a piece of thick card for the base. Cut a circle of body fabric 1in (2.5cm) bigger than the card, gather around the edge and draw up around the card circle. Sew this to the base of the body.

3 Stuff the arms to the elbows then sew around just above the stuffing line to form a joint. Lightly stuff the remaining upper arm, neaten the raw edge and sew to the doll's shoulders, making sure that the thumbs point outwards.

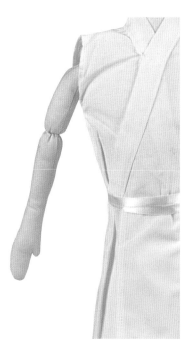

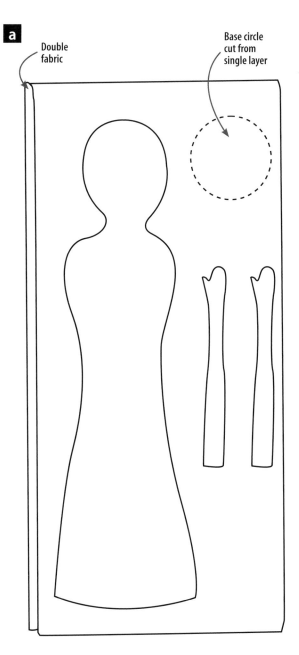

a

Double fabric

Base circle cut from single layer

TIP

When making dolls, or any stuffed toy, always sew with a small machine stitch. This will allow you to stuff the project firmly without splitting the seams.

4 Take the black hair fabric, fold in half, short ends together, and join with a ¼in (6mm) seam. Run a small gathering stitch around one edge, leaving the thread attached. Draw the hairline on the dolls head.

5 With the seam of the black fabric down the back of the head, pin the gathered edge to the hairline, easing the gathers as you go. Sew this securely in place by hand using small stitches.

6 Once sewn in place, pull the ungathered edge up over the head to reveal the face. Fill the hair evenly with stuffing, gather the top edge of hair and pull up tight and secure. Gather around the edge of the 4in (10cm) black circle, put a ball of stuffing in the centre and pull up the gathers, adding more stuffing if required, and fasten off. Sew a top knot to the back of the head to cover up the gathers on the main hair piece, take a thread up through the centre of the top knot a few times to make a dimple and fasten off (diagram **b**).

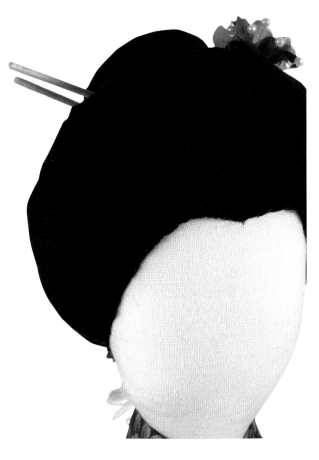

b

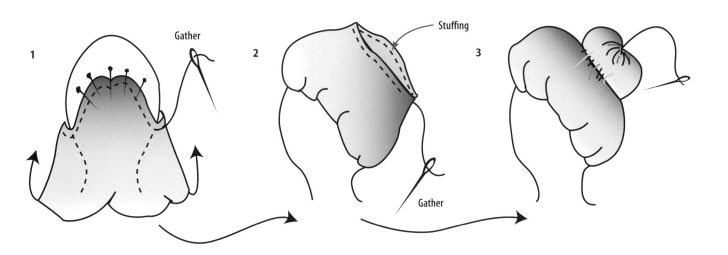

Making undergarment 'juban'

1 To make the undergarment, follow diagram **c**. Sew shoulder seams and sides leaving a 4in (10cm) opening for the armholes. Neaten armholes and turn the hem by ¼in (6mm) and neaten.

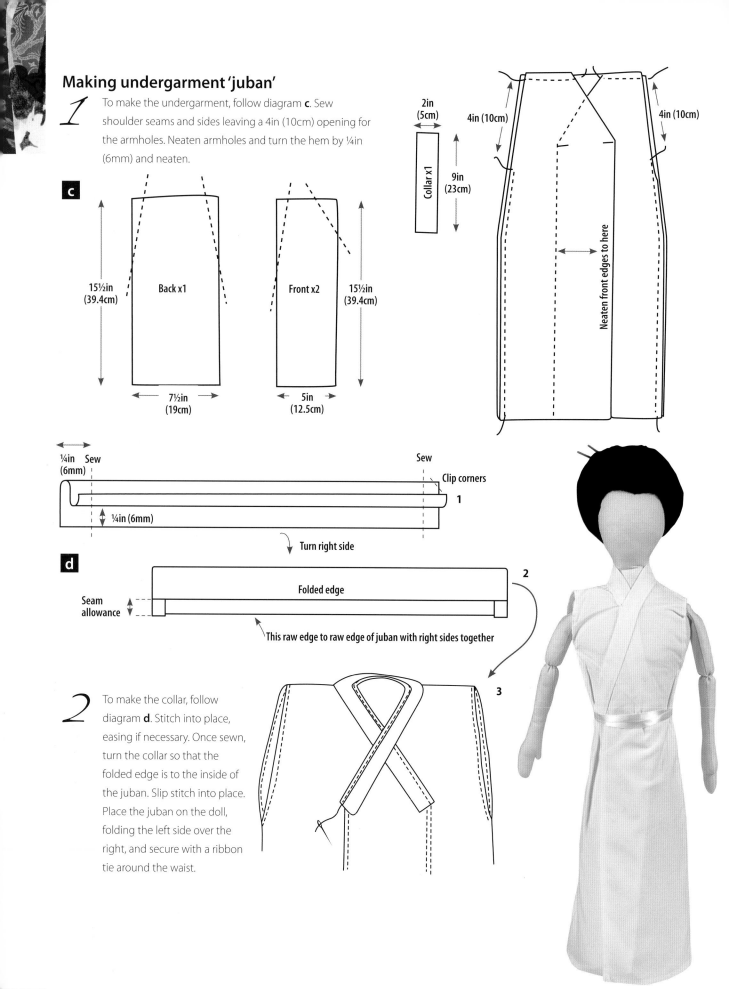

c

Back x1

15½in (39.4cm)

7½in (19cm)

Front x2

15½in (39.4cm)

5in (12.5cm)

2in (5cm)

Collar x1

9in (23cm)

4in (10cm)

4in (10cm)

Neaten front edges to here

d

¼in (6mm)

Sew

Sew

Clip corners

1

¼in (6mm)

Turn right side

Folded edge

2

Seam allowance

This raw edge to raw edge of juban with right sides together

3

2 To make the collar, follow diagram **d**. Stitch into place, easing if necessary. Once sewn, turn the collar so that the folded edge is to the inside of the juban. Slip stitch into place. Place the juban on the doll, folding the left side over the right, and secure with a ribbon tie around the waist.

Making kimono one

1 Follow diagram **e** for the block pieced kimono. From these pieces, cut shapes out as shown in diagram **f**. Sew the fronts to the back panel with right sides together, slightly sloping the seams from the neck edge to the arm edge.

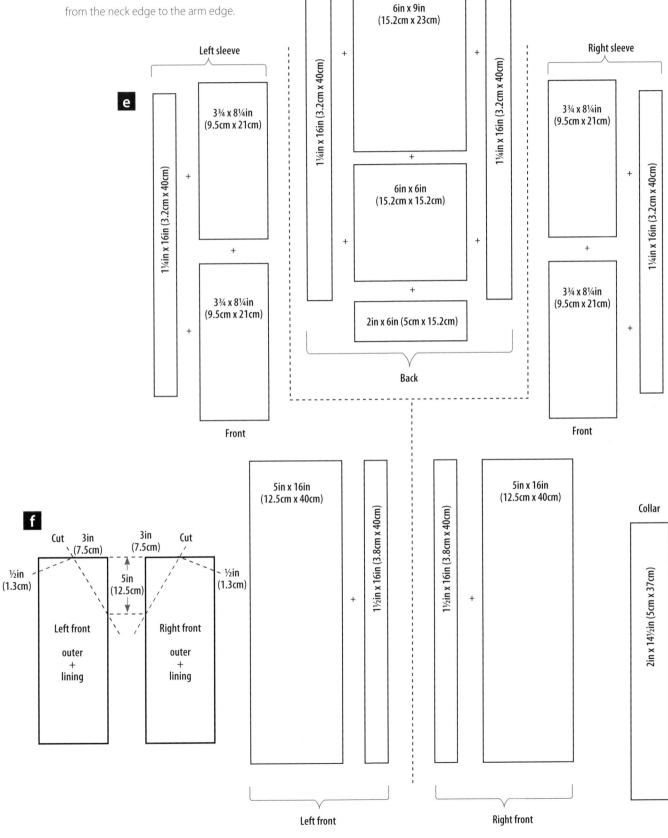

e

Left sleeve

1¼in x 16in (3.2cm x 40cm)

3¾ x 8¼in (9.5cm x 21cm)

3¾ x 8¼in (9.5cm x 21cm)

Front

1¼in x 16in (3.2cm x 40cm)

6in x 9in (15.2cm x 23cm)

6in x 6in (15.2cm x 15.2cm)

2in x 6in (5cm x 15.2cm)

1¼in x 16in (3.2cm x 40cm)

Back

Right sleeve

3¾ x 8¼in (9.5cm x 21cm)

3¾ x 8¼in (9.5cm x 21cm)

1¼in x 16in (3.2cm x 40cm)

Front

f

Cut

3in (7.5cm)

3in (7.5cm)

Cut

½in (1.3cm)

5in (12.5cm)

½in (1.3cm)

Left front
outer + lining

Right front
outer + lining

5in x 16in (12.5cm x 40cm)

1½in x 16in (3.8cm x 40cm)

1½in x 16in (3.8cm x 40cm)

5in x 16in (12.5cm x 40cm)

Collar

2in x 14½in (5cm x 37cm)

Left front

Right front

2 Position the sleeves as shown in diagram **g** and sew to the body of the kimono, leaving 4½in (11.5cm) unsewn at both ends of these seams.

3 Pin the front to the back at the side seams and sew up 10½in (26.7cm) from the bottom edge. Sew the sleeves together as shown in diagram **h**, curving the bottom corner and leaving 2½in (6.3cm) unsewn for the hand hole. Now continue with the lining instructions on page 112.

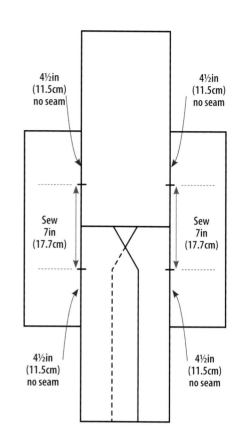

g

4½in (11.5cm) no seam

4½in (11.5cm) no seam

Sew 7in (17.7cm)

Sew 7in (17.7cm)

4½in (11.5cm) no seam

4½in (11.5cm) no seam

h

2½in (6.3cm) open

2½in (6.3cm) open

1½in (3.8cm) unsewn

10½in (26.7cm)

TIP

As with all dressmaking, press your seams open where possible, unless otherwise stated in the instructions.

The block pieced kimono one. As a finishing touch, you could turn up one bottom corner of the kimono to reveal the pretty lining beneath. Catch this in place with a few small stitches.

Making kimono two

Follow diagram **i** for the strip pieced kimono and continue with kimono construction as for kimono one, steps 1–3. Add the lining, following instructions on pages 112.

Add the lining, following instructions on pages 112.

Collar | 2in x 14½in (5cm x 36.8cm)

i

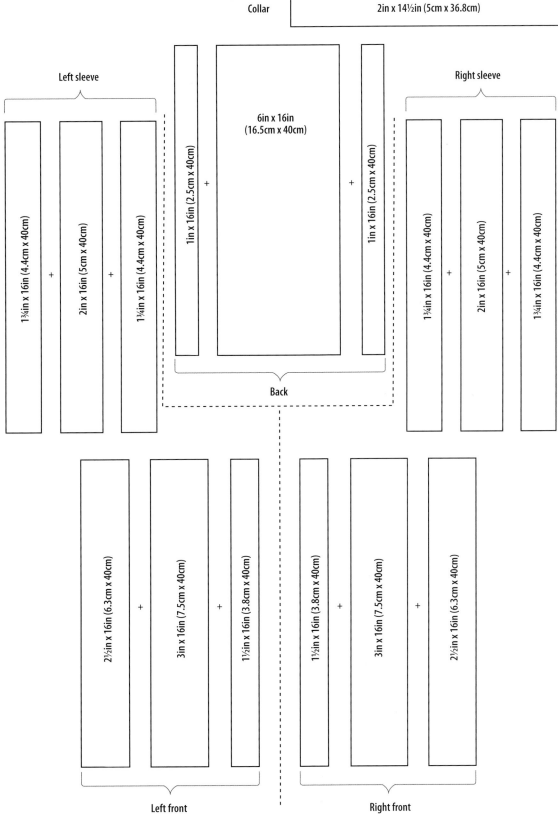

Left sleeve

1¾in x 16in (4.4cm x 40cm) + 2in x 16in (5cm x 40cm) + 1¾in x 16in (4.4cm x 40cm)

1in x 16in (2.5cm x 40cm) + 6in x 16in (16.5cm x 40cm) + 1in x 16in (2.5cm x 40cm)

Back

Right sleeve

1¾in x 16in (4.4cm x 40cm) + 2in x 16in (5cm x 40cm) + 1¾in x 16in (4.4cm x 40cm)

Left front

2½in x 16in (6.3cm x 40cm) + 3in x 16in (7.5cm x 40cm) + 1½in x 16in (3.8cm x 40cm)

Right front

1½in x 16in (3.8cm x 40cm) + 3in x 16in (7.5cm x 40cm) + 2½in x 16in (6.3cm x 40cm)

FABRIC CHOICE

We suggest that you use fabrics from one collection, with a main larger patterned fabric for the centre back of the kimono. Use contrasting fabrics for piecing the front and sleeves. Try to be bold with your colours but keep the contrasts within the limit of the main fabric.

If your Geisha has been made for a special birthday gift, why not make the headdress from fresh wired flowers such as jasmine, or any small, scented flowers?

Kimono lining

1 Sew the two fronts to the back panel at the shoulders with the slanting seams as the kimono. With right sides together, sew linings to the outer fabric, starting at the collar's lowest point and finishing at the opposite point on the other front. Clip corners and turn lining to the inside of the kimono. Press well.

2 Make up sleeve linings by folding the strips in half and sewing as for the outer sleeves. Attach each lining to a sleeve, right sides together, at the hand holes (see diagram **j**). Sew together with a ¼in (6mm) seam, then push the lining through the hole and press well.

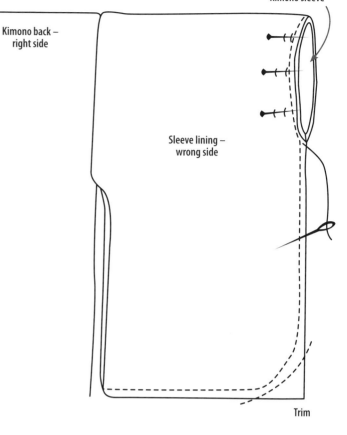

j

Kimono back – right side

Sleeve lining – wrong side

Kimono sleeve

Trim

3 With the lining outermost, slip stitch sleeve linings to body lining and neaten all other edges. Make up the collar as for the juban (page 106) and attach in the same way.

4 Dress the doll in her kimono, making sure that the left front is wrapped over the right front. Pin in place while you make the obi.

Making the obi

1 Cut two pieces of fabric 2½in x 44in (6.3cm x 112cm). The outer fabric can be the silk, lined with a contrasting fabric, or you can do both in silk.

2 Sew together leaving one short end open, clip the corners and then turn right side out and press. Gently insert the 1¾in x 6in (4.4cm x 15.2cm) piece of pelmet Vilene so that it lies in the middle of the sash. This makes the obi nice and rigid. Neaten the open end with a slip stitch.

3 Secure the obi around the doll's upper waist with one firm knot at the back. Now tie the cord length around the obi (this is known as the obi-jime) and secure with a reef knot at the back. Complete the obi by tying into a bow at the back (butterfly obi).

TIP
Inserting the pelmet Vilene into the obi can be a bit tricky. Slightly fold the Vilene in half lengthways and slide into the obi. When centralised, flatten and press.

Finishing

All that is left to complete your beautiful geisha is to embellish the hair. Here you can use cocktail sticks and hang threaded beads from them or you can make a small floral hairpiece and attach it to the hair with either glue or a few tight stitches. The face is left blank as there are no contours to follow or give depth to, but you may add features if you wish.

Techniques

Binding a quilt or cushion

1 Join 2½in (6.3cm) strips together on the cross to form one long strip (wrong sides together). Cut off the excess and press seams to one side (see diagram **a**).

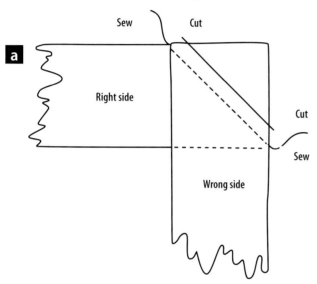

a

Sew   Cut

Right side

Cut

Sew

Wrong side

2 Fold the left hand end of the strip, as shown in diagram **b**, and then press the strip in half along the entire length.

b

1

Fold

Wrong side

2

Right side

3 With the right side of your quilt or cushion facing up, place the binding against one edge a few inches off a corner. Leave a tail of binding (just an inch or so). Start sewing a ¼in (6mm) seam clockwise. Stop and cast off ¼in (6mm) from the corner (see diagram **c**).

c

'Tail'

¼in (6mm)

Raw edge

4 Fold the binding away from the corner, creating a 45-degree angle, with all raw edges in an even line, as in diagram **d**.

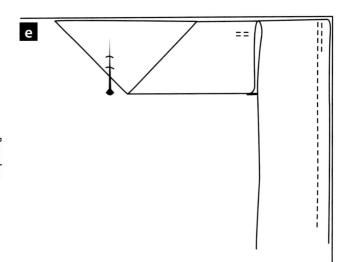

d

Raw edges

45°

Raw edges

5 Fold the binding back on itself, making sure the fold is level with the edge. Reverse stitch over the edge and then continue down to within a ¼in (6mm) of the next corner. When all corners are complete, feed the end into the folded tail and stitch over, as in diagram **e**.

e

== ==

||

6 Turn the folded edge of the binding to the back and slip stitch in place, creating mitre corners as you go, as in diagram **f**.

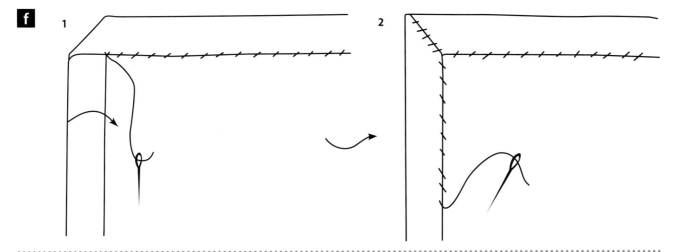

f

1

2

Sleeves and tab tops

When making sleeves for wall hangings, measure across the top and bottom of your hanging, cut a piece of matching fabric 2in (5cm) shorter than the measurement and 5in (12.5cm) deep, turn in the long ends by ½in (1.3cm) and sew down. Turn in ½in (1.3cm) on the short ends and sew down. Pin to the top and bottom of the hanging and slipstitch into place.

Tab tops depend on the width of your hanging: for a wide one make five tabs, for a shorter one three tabs will do. Cut matching fabric 8in (20cm) by 5in (12.5cm), fold down ½in (1.3cm) along one long edge and fold over other edge to line up with opposite raw edge. Press over the already turned edge and sew along to hold together. Do this three/five times depending on how many you need. Measure equal distance and pin on to the back of the wall hanging after you have finished off the binding. Remember to neaten edges by turning under approx ¾in (2cm).

Equipment

There are many gadgets and gizmos on the market these days for every aspect of patchwork, quilting and general sewing. We have listed below the most essential items needed to complete any of the projects in this book. Wherever possible, it is always preferable to purchase the best you can afford. Cheaper products may save you money in the short term but will not necessarily last very long.

Rotary cutter

You have a choice of 28mm, 45mm or 60mm blades – the 45mm is about the most versatile size. Fiskars and Olfa are both notable makes. Replacement blades are always available.

Rulers

We prefer to use the 6½in x 24½in (16cm x 60cm) perspex rulers, wide enough to keep your whole hand safely away from your rotary cutting blade. They also have useful 30-, 45- and 60-degree angle marks.

Cutting mat

The most useful size is 17in x 24in (43.2cm x 61cm). Make sure you store it somewhere flat, out of the sun, as it can buckle in strong sunlight, never to be flat again.

Iron

A normal domestic iron is all that is needed. Sometimes steam is required but for most patchwork a dry iron is adequate. Steam can distort and stretch cotton fabrics, especially those cut on the cross.

Baking parchment/greaseproof paper

An essential item when using fusible webs (i.e. Bondaweb) to protect your iron and ironing board. It is also useful for tracing designs and templates.

Sewing machine

It would be an ideal world if we could all have top of the range sewing machines but that isn't always possible. All the projects in this book can be easily produced using a simple machine with variable stitch length, a good zig-zag facility that will satin stitch and be able to either drop or cover the feed dogs.

TIP

Keep your machine clean by de-fluffing regularly (see your instruction manual) and fit a new needle at the beginning of each new project.

Quarter inch seam foot

Most machine manufacturers produce a quarter inch foot these days. Some machines have a presser foot that is just slightly bigger and this is fine for most projects.

Darning foot

Essential for free machine quilting and embroidery.

Scissors

A good pair of scissors is a delight to use. A pair of shears, hobby (round ended) and embroidery are essential in any sewing box. Keep safely away from hands that may use them inappropriately!

Needles

Recommended are **household assorted** for all general sewing, **betweens** for quilting, size 8 is the biggest and size 12 the smallest, **milliners straws** for tacking.

Quilters ¼

This is a ¼in (6mm) plastic rod, very useful for measuring accurately your ¼in (6mm) seam allowances.

HB pencil

For marking seam allowances on the reverse of your fabrics. Always keep it sharp.

Thimble

There are many thimbles available, metal, leather and plastic. Always try on for size wherever possible. For those who can't use a thimble but hate sore fingers, Thimblets are sticky reuseable pads that help to prevent sore fingers.

Threads

A minefield of choice. Basic 50 gauge cotton is most useful for piecing your patchwork, either by hand or machine. Glazed quilting thread for hand quilting. Plain or variegated 40 gauge threads for machine quilting. Rayon threads for decorative machining.

Wadding

There are so many different types of wadding (or batting) on the market now, low loft for machine quilting, wool for the ultimate in hand quilting, compressed polyester wadding for bags and wall hangings, hypoallergenic alpaca and cotton.

TIP

When buying wadding for a specific project, ask your friendly quilt shop to recommend the most appropriate. One rule of thumb is the more you pay for your wadding the less quilting you will need to do.

Markers

There are markers for every occasion. Blue 'washaway' pens will mark most fabrics, always pre-test on a fabric scrap first and wash away in clean tepid water. Do not iron the lines as heat will fix them and you will never get them out.

Chaco liner is a lipstick sized container with a small metal wheel that dispenses a fine line of powdered chalk, available in different colours. The line disappears easily and is ideal for machining straight lines.

Silver, yellow or white chalk pencils are ideal for marking darker fabrics. Keep the point of the pencil sharp and try to draw a disjointed line.

Spray starch

When you have cotton fabrics of varying weights it sometimes helps to use spray starch. It gives the fabric extra body and helps to stabilise it.

505 temporary adhesive

When you need to layer fabric and wadding, 505 spray saves having to tack or pin the layers together. It is only temporary and easily washes out.

Dressmaker's carbon paper

One of the easier ways of transferring quilting lines to your projects.

Templates

These are all the templates that you will need for the projects in the book. Use when indicated in the relevant instructions. Where they need to be enlarged, this is easily done with a photocopier.

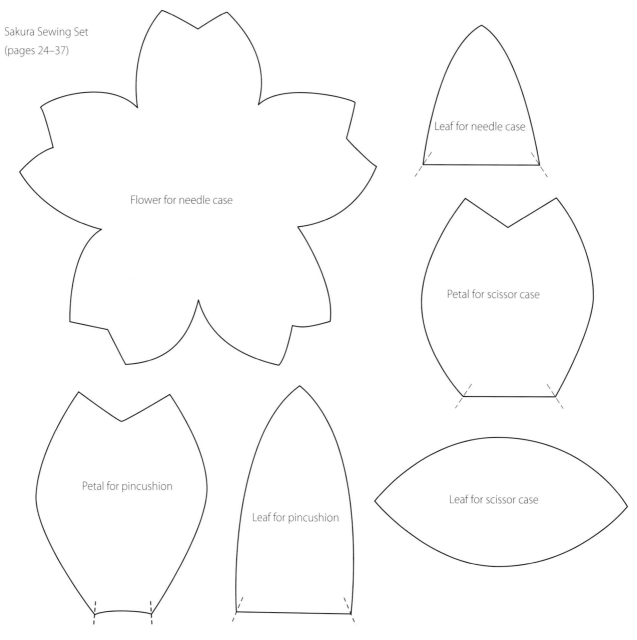

Sakura Sewing Set
(pages 24–37)

Flower for needle case

Leaf for needle case

Petal for scissor case

Petal for pincushion

Leaf for pincushion

Leaf for scissor case

Enlarge by 125%

Kinkakuji Wallhanging (pages 44–49)

top and bottom panels

Enlarge by 125%

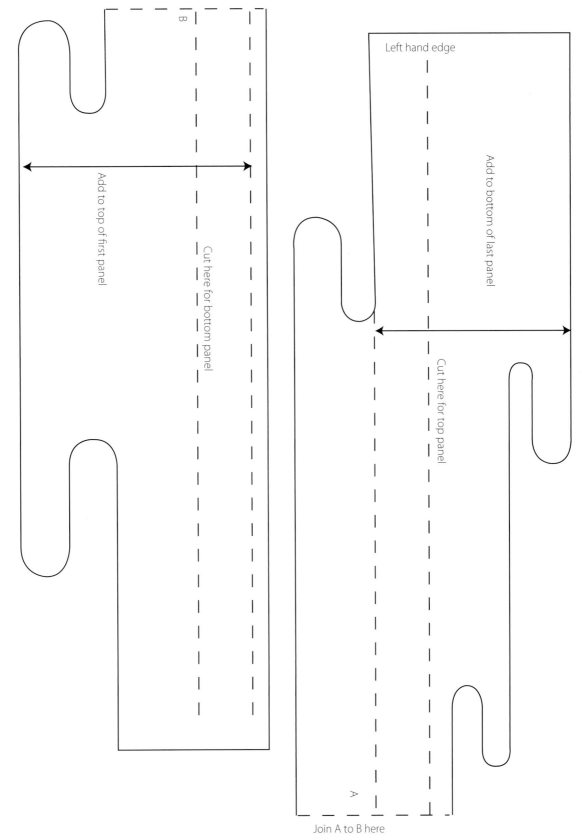

Add to top of first panel

Cut here for bottom panel

B

Left hand edge

Add to bottom of last panel

Cut here for top panel

A

Join A to B here

Blossom branches
(ideal for borders)

Enlarge by 125%

Enlarge by 125%

Cherry blossom
(sakura)

Maple leaves
(kaede)

Appliqué templates for Shoji Screen
Wallhanging (pages 72–79)

Fabric 3

Fabric 1

1

2

Fabric 2

4

Fabric 1   3

5

4

3

2

1

9

10

11

3

2

5

1

4

6

7

8

Fabric 1   Fabric 2

1

2

Numbers give placement order

Enlarge by 125%

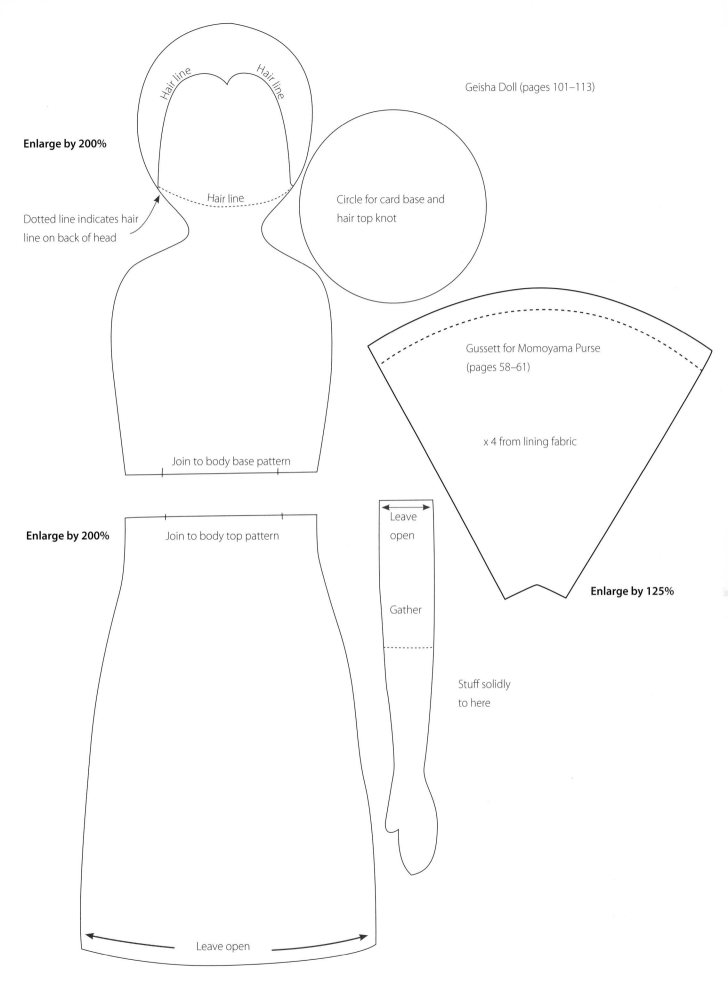

Enlarge by 200%

Hair line

Hair line

Hair line

Dotted line indicates hair
line on back of head

Circle for card base and
hair top knot

Join to body base pattern

Gussett for Momoyama Purse
(pages 58–61)

x 4 from lining fabric

Enlarge by 125%

Enlarge by 200%

Join to body top pattern

Leave
open

Gather

Stuff solidly
to here

Leave open

Suppliers

Europe

Stof A/S
Hammershusvej 2c
DK – 7400 Herning
Denmark
www.stof.dk

UK

Step By Step Patchwork Centre
Barnstaple Road
South Molton
Devon, EX36 3RD
www.stepbystep-quilts.co.uk

Concord Fabrics (UK) Ltd
Makower Craft
118 Greys Road
Henley on Thames
Oxon, RG9 1QW
www.makoweruk.com

Creative Grids (UK)Ltd
Unit 1J, Peckleton Lane Business Park
Peckleton Common Road
Peckleton
Leicestershire, LE9 9JU
www.creativegrids.com

EQS
11 Iliffe House
Iliffe Avenue
Leicester, LE2 5LS
www.eqsuk.com

Marathon Threads Ltd
Marathon House
Tavistock Avenue
Ripley
Derbyshire, DE5 3SE
www.marathonthreads.co.uk

Timeless Treasures (UK) Ltd
Unit 3, Halifax House
Coronation Road
High Wycombe
Bucks, HP12 3SE
www.ttfabrics.eu

Winbourne Fabrics Ltd
Unit 3a, Forge Way
Brown Lees Industrial Estate
Knypersley
Stoke on Trent, S78 7DN
www.winbofabrics.co.uk

USA

Kona Bay Fabrics
1637 Kahai Street
Honolulu
Hawaii 96819
www.konabay.com

Moda Fabrics
13800 Hutton Drive
Dallas, TX 75324,
www.modahome.com

Timeless Treasures Ltd
483 Broadway
New York, NY 10013,
www.ttfabrics.com

Hoffman California Fabrics
25792 Obrero Drive
Mission Viejo, CA 92691
www.hoffmanfabrics.com

The Warm Company
954 East Union Street
Seattle, WA 98122
www.warmcompany.com

About the Authors

Julia Davis and Anne Muxworthy have run Step by Step Patchwork Centre since 1999. This came about as Anne had empty premises with an idea for a patchwork shop and Julia taught patchwork and quilting at the local college and at home. Both are experienced quilters and have a wide knowledge of fabrics. They specialise in Oriental style fabrics, which are sourced from Kona Bay Fabrics, Hoffman, Moda and Timeless Treasures.

As well as taking these lovely fabrics to shows, Julia and Anne enjoy sharing their knowledge on how to use them by running classes and workshops. The shop is always busy and there is an ever-growing mail order service, a website and group visits. They can also provide a 'mobile shop', offering most of their range to groups within a 100-mile radius. For more information on Julia, Anne and the Step by Step Patchwork Centre, see the contact details on page 126.

Acknowledgments

We would both like to thank our husbands, Bernard and Robert for their full support and encouragement and having late dinners!

Our sincere thanks to Linda, Sue and Sally, who read through all of our instructions and tested some of our projects to make sure they worked well.

And finally, to all our ladies, who have been behind us all the way with their enthusiasm and full support.

To all of you, we thank you!

Index

Page numbers in **bold** indicate a Tip; those in *italic*, a template.